Most-Used Shorthand Wo
and Phrases

GREGG
Most-Used Shorthand Words and Phrases

Third Edition

(including transcription previously published separately as *Gregg Graded Dictation*)

John R. Gregg, Louis A. Leslie
Charles E. Zoubek, Ernest W. Crockett

McGRAW-HILL Book Company (UK) Limited

LONDON · New York · St Louis · San Francisco
Auckland · Bogatá · Düsseldorf · Johannesburg · Madrid
Mexico · Montreal · New Delhi · Panama · Paris · São Paulo
Singapore · Sydney · Tokyo · Toronto

Most-Used Shorthand Words and Phrases

Third Edition

07 094413 X

PRINTED AND BOUND IN GREAT BRITAIN

PREFACE

Most-Used Shorthand Words and Phrases, Third Edition, contains the shorthand outlines for more than 4,000 words and more than 1,800 phrases selected on the basis of usefulness and frequency.

The words are selected from the first 10,000 words in order of frequency in the Horn-Peterson *Basic Vocabulary of Business Letters*. Many of these 10,000 words, being simple derivative forms such as those ending in *-ing*, *-ed*, *-s*, etc., which the shorthand writer can immediately construct for himself when the prime form is given, are not included. Thus the 4,000-odd words contained herein comprise most of the stenographic value of the 10,000 most frequently used words in business dictation. The phrases are selected from the 3,536 most frequent phrases listed by Charles E. Zoubek in an analysis of more than 250,000 running words of business-letter material.

In addition to the word lists and phrase lists, this volume presents in shorthand, at the end of each Lesson from Lesson 3 onwards, a series of sentences or short letters based on the vocabulary of the preceding lessons. These provide further material for practice in shorthand reading and writing.

Each numbered paragraph in *Most-Used Shorthand Words and Phrases* contains those shorthand outlines (from the above-mentioned sources) that are constructed in accordance with the correspondingly numbered paragraph in the *Gregg Shorthand Manual Simplified*, Second Edition. The book is thus designed as a companion volume to the *Manual*. (See also footnote on page 7.)

There are alternative methods by which this material can be used to consolidate your knowledge of the shorthand principles and to develop your skill in applying them. The method recommended is to use each lesson of *Most-Used Shorthand Words and Phrases* immediately after each corresponding lesson in the *Manual* has been studied—including the Reading and Writing Practice of that lesson. Treat each paragraph in the way that you treated the corresponding paragraph of the *Manual*: cover the printed words in order to read the shorthand forms without their aid; then uncover to check the accuracy of your reading; finally, write the shorthand forms, speaking the words aloud as you do so. Deal similarly with the phrase lists; and use the Reading and Writing Practice section in the same way that you studied the similar section in the *Manual.*

These methods of study are equally suitable if you prefer, or if your teacher prefers, that the material be used for revision practice immediately following individual paragraphs or individual complete chapters of the *Manual*, or as a general revision after the whole *Manual* has been studied.

Throughout your work on *Most-Used Shorthand Words and Phrases* the aim should be, not specially to memorize shorthand outlines (though some memorizing is likely to occur), but chiefly to gain skill in the application of the outline-building principles of the system—skill that will enable you to construct without hesitation the outlines for unfamiliar expressions as these are encountered.

Graded Dictation

Transcriptions of the Reading and Writing sections of Lessons 3 to 45 are given at the end of this book. These were previously published separately under the title *Gregg Graded Dictation.*

CHAPTER ONE

Lesson I

***3.** *A, S-Z, F, V*

face — phase — safe — save — saves — say

5. *E, N, M*

easy — fee — fees — sea — see — sees

knee — navy — sane — scene — seem — vain

aim — main — may — me — mean — same

6. *T, D*

east — faced — feet — meat — meet — neat — seat

stain — stay — steam — tea — team — aid — day

deed — feed — made — need — saved — seed — stayed

* Paragraph serial numbers are those of the *Gregg Shorthand Manual Simplified*, Second Edition.

7. *O, R, L*

foe	dear	deal
know	drain	fail
no	drove	feel
note	fair	late
sew	free	lead
snow	freight	leave
so	near	low
stove	rate	mail
stow	road	real
toe	trade	relay
vote	treat	retail
zone	wrote	steal

8. *H*

hair	hate	heat
haste	hear	heed

9. Omission of minor vowels

dealer	heater	notary
Easter	later	reader
even	meter	season
favour	motor	steamer
hasten	nearer	total

Lesson 2

13. *S-Z, P, B*

days, knows, least, means, niece, notes, readers, seems

hope, open, paid, paper, pays, people, place, prepare

able, base, better, blame, boats, brief, labour, neighbours

14. *K, G*

broke, came, claim, clear, close

cream, keys, sake, taken, gain

game, gave, girls, grade, grow

15. *Sh, Ch, J*

shade, shaped, shares, sheep, show

chains, cheaper, chose, each, reached

age, changed, page, range, storage

16. Long *I*

buy		hide	
cried		iron	
drive		light	
dry		might	
dye		night	
files		obliged	
height		rely	

rise
slight
styles
tire
tried
type
vital

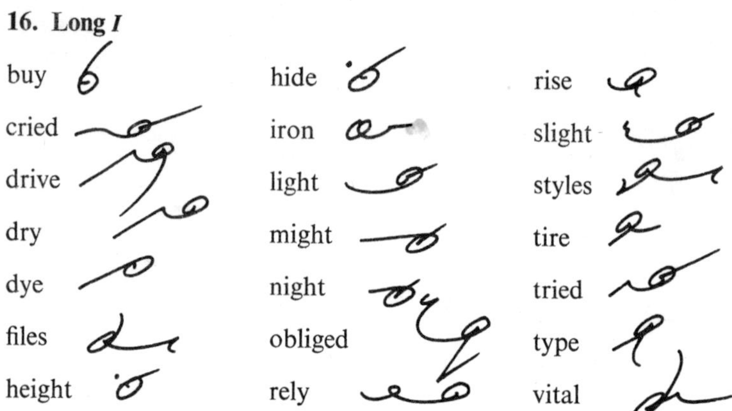

Lesson 3

18. Additional sounds of *a*; dot for *-ing*

add	alarm	aiming
advice	arm	bearing
agree	army	casting
appear	bargain	charming
arrive	charged	evening
attached	far	grading
average	farms	greeting
capital	harm	heating
habit	large	lining
had	mark	making
has	star	trading
man	starts	trying

10

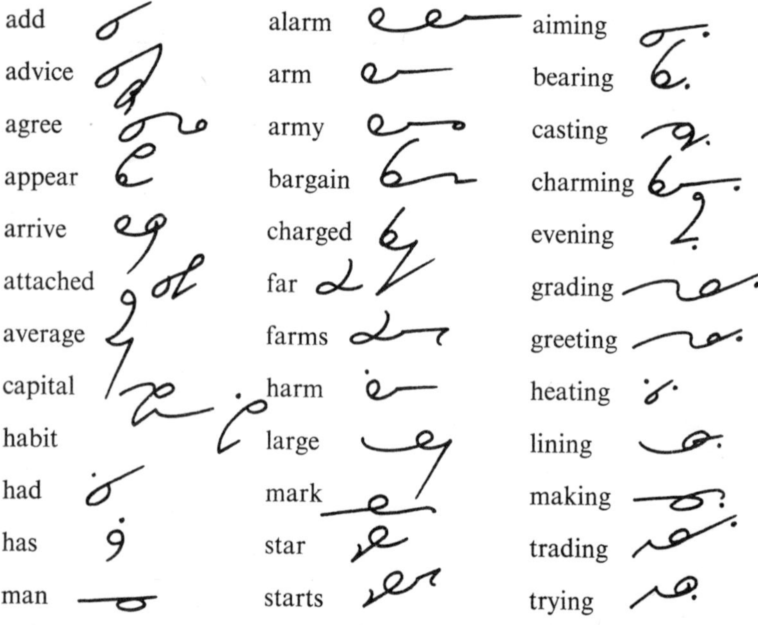

19. Additional sounds of *e*

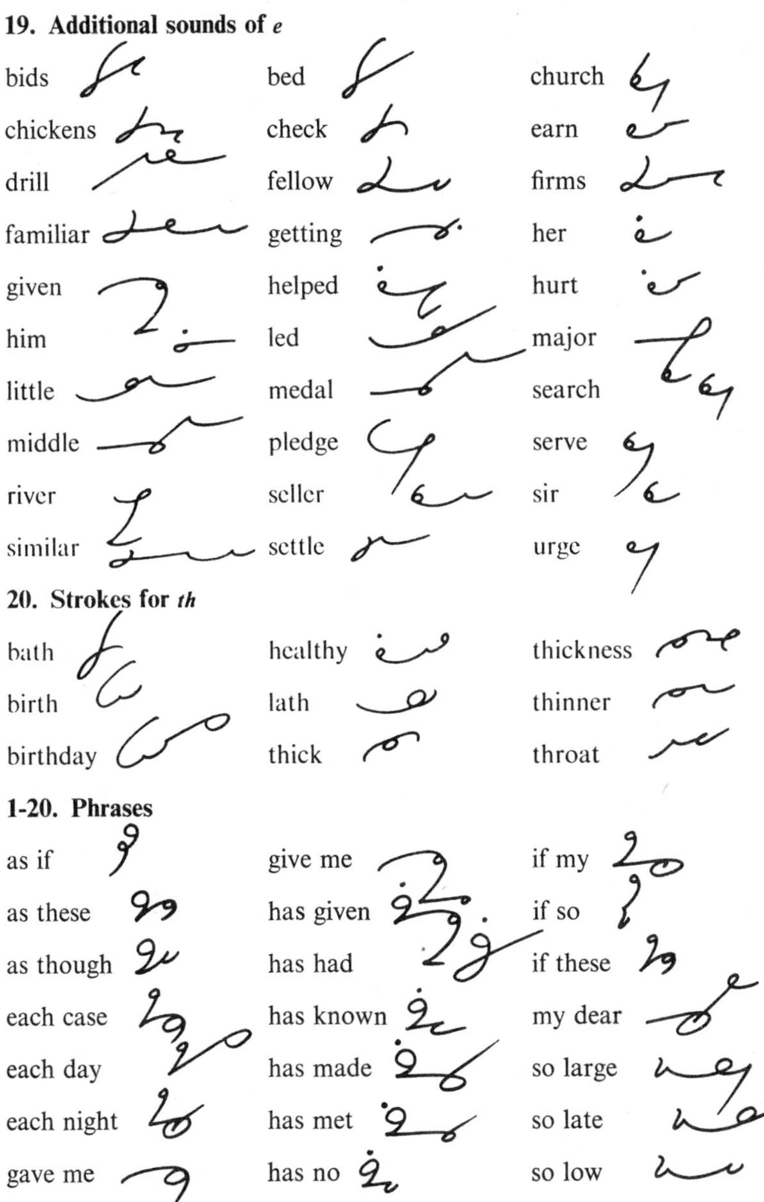

20. Strokes for *th*

1-20. Phrases

21. Brief Forms

a	goes	its
ago	going	more
am	good	not
an	goods	our
are	he	ours
at	hour	the
can	hours	well
cannot	I	will
can't	in	wills
go	it	would

22. Phrases

are not	here are	these are
at least	at the	at these
can go	as good	good deal
he came	he felt	he lives
he can	he gets	he made
he can't	he knows	he may
he drove	he left	he needs

he reaches	he will	he will say
he said	he will not	he would

I am	I get	I ran
I came	I give	I reached
I can	I guess	I read
I can say	I know	I realize
I cannot	I left	I said
I cannot say	I live	I say
I can see	I make	I see
I cannot see	I may	I will
I can't	I mean	I will not
I drove	I met	I will see
I fear	I might	I would
I feel	I need	I would not
I gave	I notice	I wrote

in case	in its	in the
in it	in our	in these

as it	if it	it will
as it will	it has	it will not

as the — has the — make the

ask the — if the — realize the

had not — has not — might not

as well — well known — will pay

so well — will not — will see

Reading and Writing Practice

14

15

16

Lesson 4

24. Short sound of *o*

adopt	crossed	loss
block	dock	lost
blotter	dog	lot
bronze	drop	mob
catalogue	hop	model
clock	hospital	moderate
co-operate	hot	mop
copies	job	observe
copper	jobber	occur
cottage	lobby	occurrence
crop	lock	odd
cross	logs	off

offer	pocket	shop
offset	popular	soft
often	rob	spot
oftener	robbery	stock
operate	rock	stop
opposite	rod	top

Aw

abroad	caught	laws
absorb	cause	ought
bought	caused	raw
broad	clause	saw
broadcast	daughter	sought
broader	draw	talked
brought	jaw	taught

24. Phrases

across the	he saw	I talked
has taught	he talked	I thought
he lost	I saw	off the

25. Brief Forms

be	by	have
before	could	herewith
but	for	his

is
of
put
shall
ship
their
there
thereby
therefore
therein
which
with

25-26. Phrases

can be
cannot be
can't be
he can be
he will be
he will not be
he would be
I can be
I cannot be
I can't be
I may be
I will be
I would be
if it will be
it will be
it will not be
may be
may not be
might be
might not be
need be
need not be
she may be
will be
will not be
would be
would not be

by it
by its
by me
by the
by these
by which

could be
could have
could not
could not be
he could
he could not
he could see
I could be
I could have
I could not
I could say
I could see

for his
for it
for its
for me
for my
for our
for the
for their
for these
for which
for which the
before the

can have
have given
have had
have made
have not
he will have
he would have
I could have
I have
I have had
I have made
I have not
I have tried
I may have
I will have
I would have
it will have
may have
might have
will have
would have

as it is
he is
he is not
he is the
here is
if it is
in his
is it
is not
is the
is there
it is
on his
she is
she is not

of his
of it
of its
of our
of ours
of the
of their
of these
of which

I shall	I shall make	shall be
I shall be	I shall not	shall not
I shall have	I shall see	shall not be
as there	if there will	there may be
as there is	there are	there will
if there are	there is	there will be
if there is	there may	there would be
with him	with the	with which
with our	with these	with which the
in which	on which the	which may
in which the	which is	which may be
on which	which is the	which means

Reading and Writing Practice

1

2

3

4

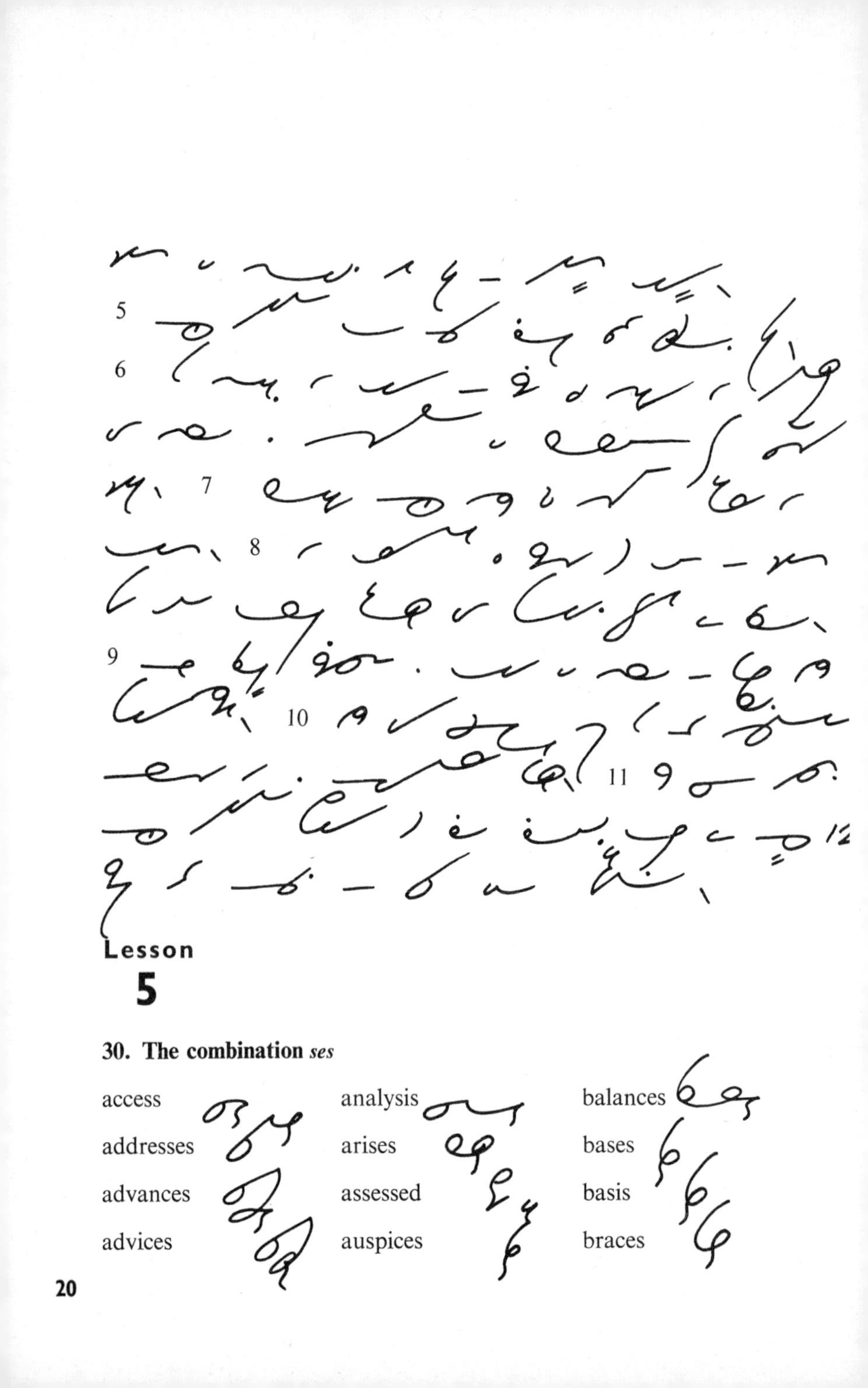

5

6

7

8

9

10

11

12

Lesson 5

30. The combination *ses*

access	analysis	balances
addresses	arises	bases
advances	assessed	basis
advices	auspices	braces

cases
causes
census
chances
classes
clauses
closes
courses
criticism
faces
finances
glasses
leases
lenses
losses
mattresses
necessitate
necessity
notices
nurses
passes
phases
pieces
places
premises
presses
prices
releases
says
senses
services
sister
sizes
sources
spaces
versus

31. *To* in phrases

as to be
has to be
is to be
to balance
to be
to bear
to beat
to bite
to blame
to borrow
to break
to burn
to buy
to change
to charge
to check
to face
to fail
to fall
to farm
to feel
to fill
to finance
to finish
to fit
to fly
to follow
to have
to park
to pass

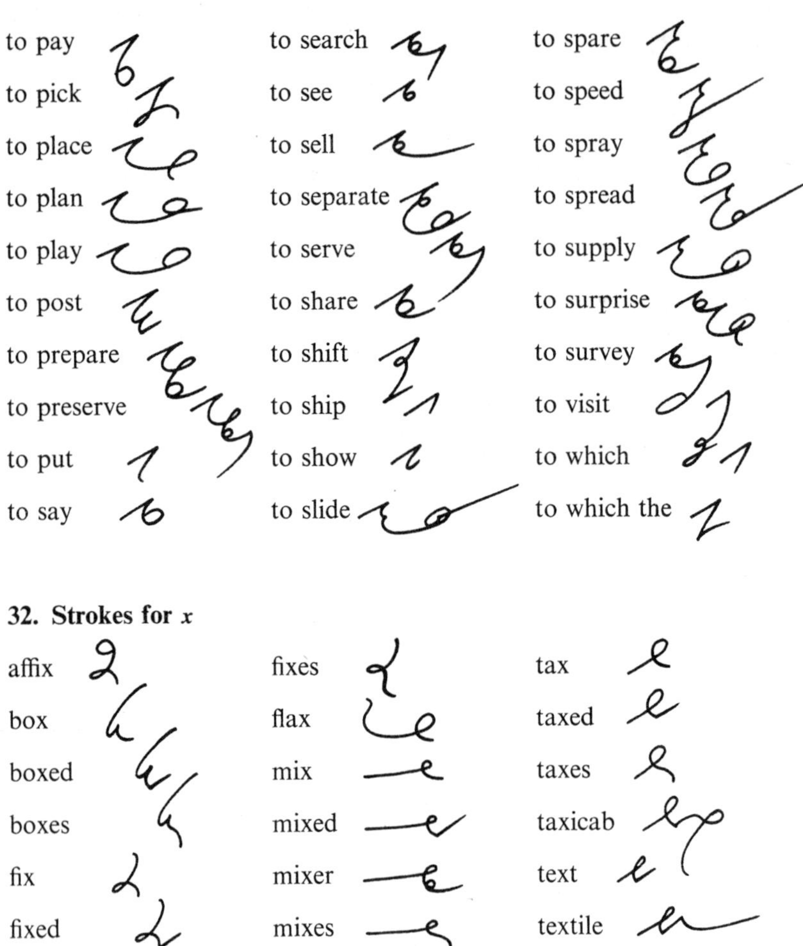

to pay	to search	to spare
to pick	to see	to speed
to place	to sell	to spray
to plan	to separate	to spread
to play	to serve	to supply
to post	to share	to surprise
to prepare	to shift	to survey
to preserve	to ship	to visit
to put	to show	to which
to say	to slide	to which the

32. Strokes for *x*

affix	fixes	tax
box	flax	taxed
boxed	mix	taxes
boxes	mixed	taxicab
fix	mixer	text
fixed	mixes	textile

Reading and Writing Practice

1 2 6. 3

Lesson 6

36. Circles inside curves

At beginning or end of curve

apply arm cry

again art error

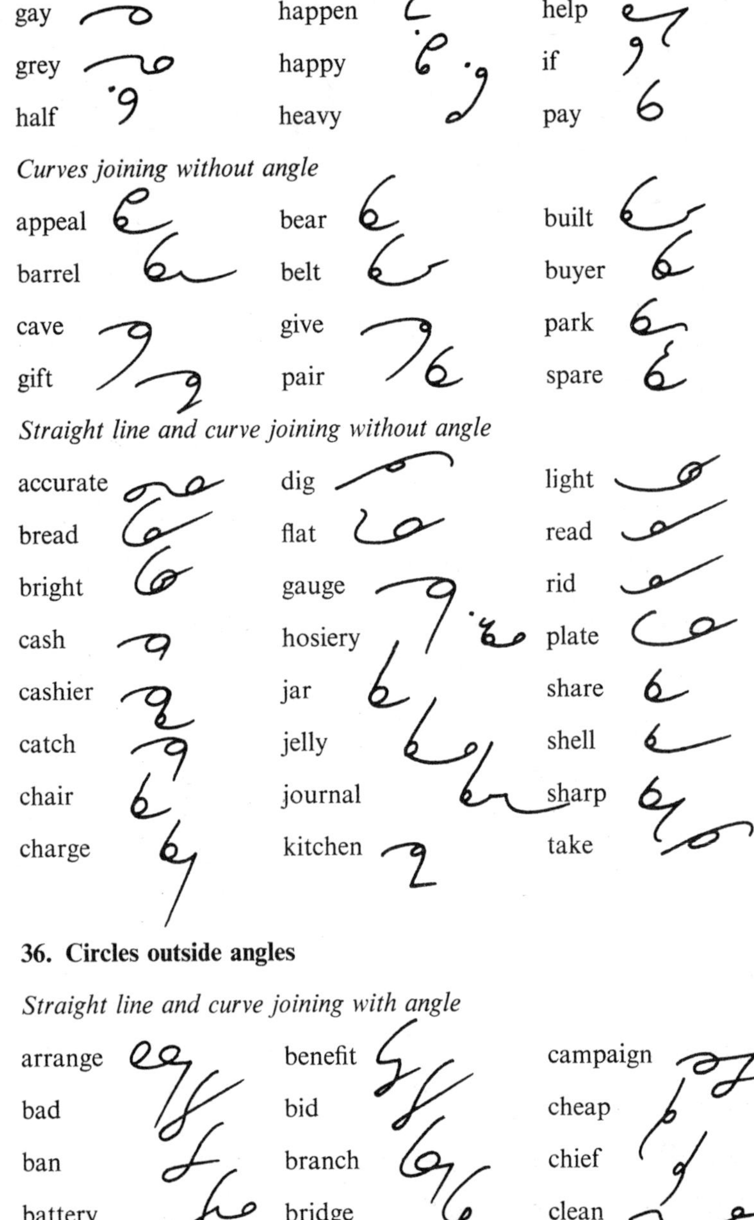

gay happen help
grey happy if
half heavy pay

Curves joining without angle

appeal bear built
barrel belt buyer
cave give park
gift pair spare

Straight line and curve joining without angle

accurate dig light
bread flat read
bright gauge rid
cash hosiery plate
cashier jar share
catch jelly shell
chair journal sharp
charge kitchen take

36. Circles outside angles

Straight line and curve joining with angle

arrange benefit campaign
bad bid cheap
ban branch chief
battery bridge clean

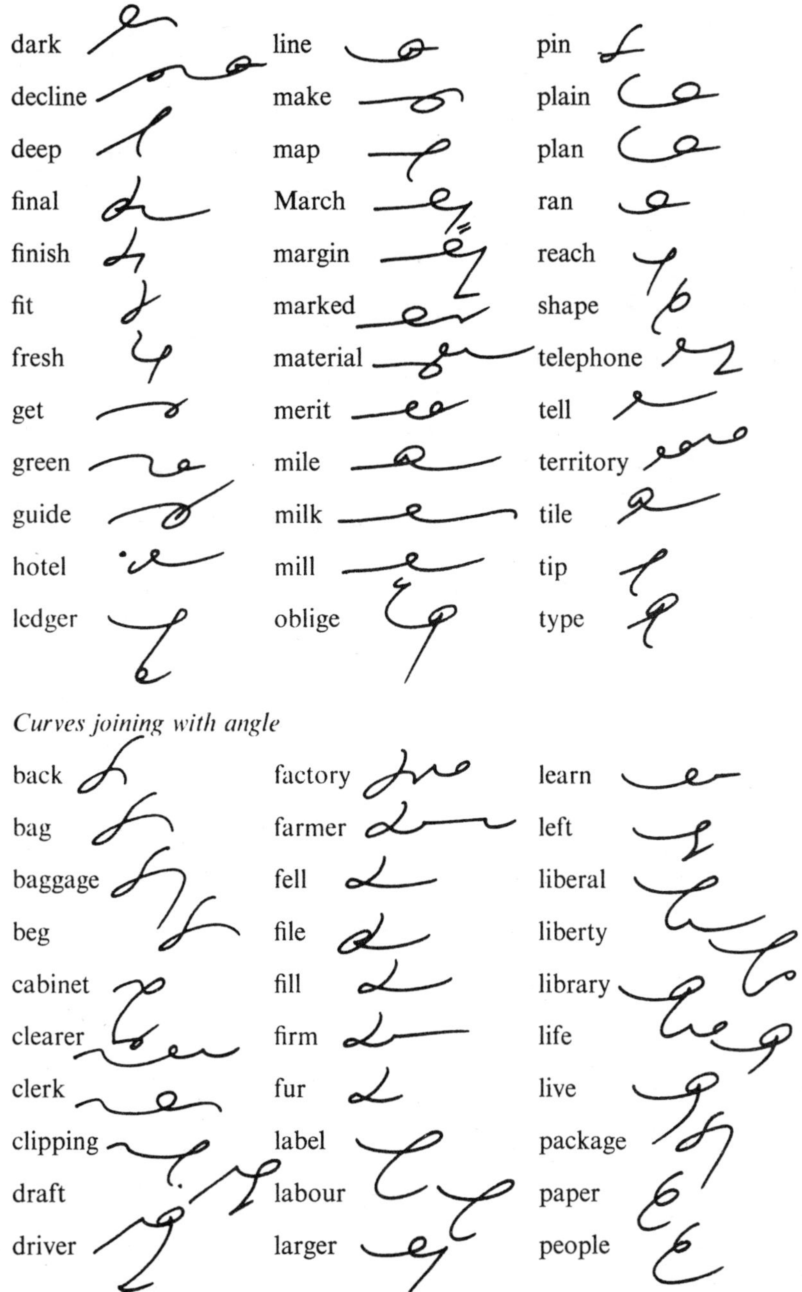
dark
decline
deep
final
finish
fit
fresh
get
green
guide
hotel
ledger
line
make
map
March
margin
marked
material
merit
mile
milk
mill
oblige
pin
plain
plan
ran
reach
shape
telephone
tell
territory
tile
tip
type
Curves joining with angle
back
bag
baggage
beg
cabinet
clearer
clerk
clipping
draft
driver
factory
farmer
fell
file
fill
firm
fur
label
labour
larger
learn
left
liberal
liberty
library
life
live
package
paper
people

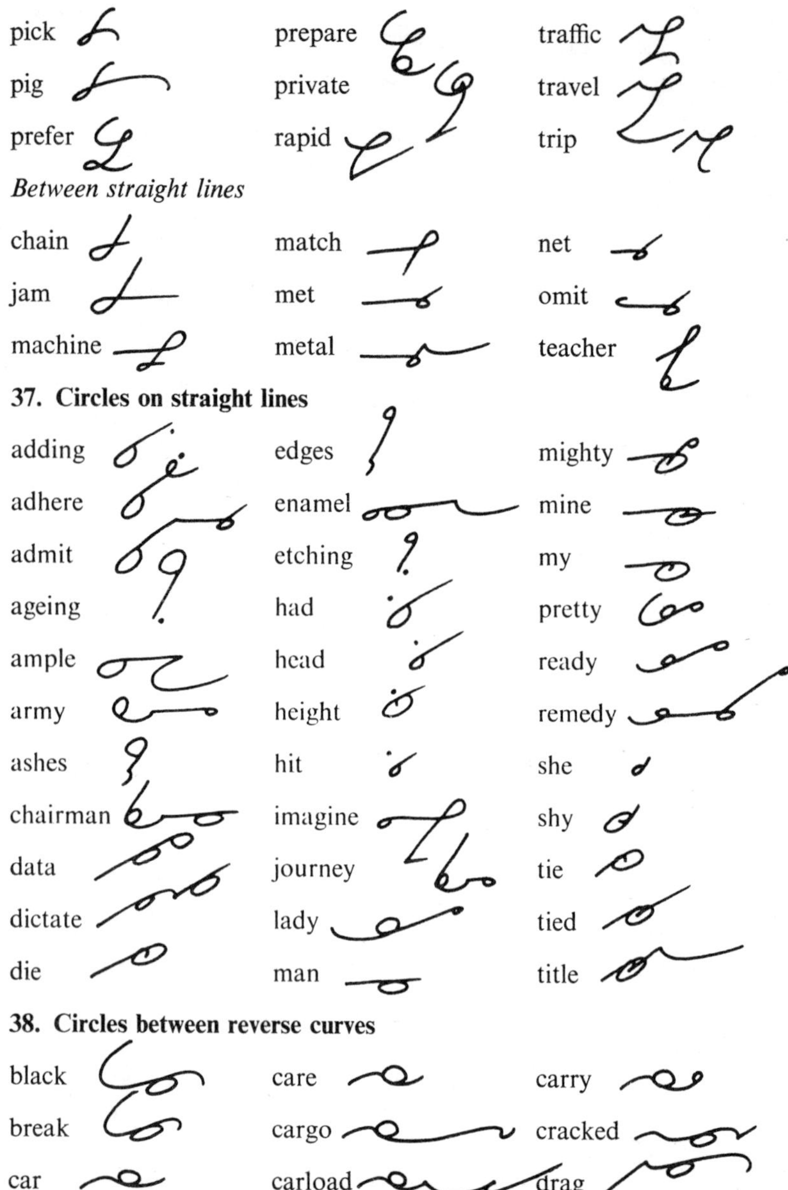

pick pig prefer

prepare private rapid

traffic travel trip

Between straight lines

chain jam machine

match met metal

net omit teacher

37. Circles on straight lines

adding adhere admit ageing ample army ashes chairman data dictate die

edges enamel etching had head height hit imagine journey lady man

mighty mine my pretty ready remedy she shy tie tied title

38. Circles between reverse curves

black break car

care cargo carload

carry cracked drag

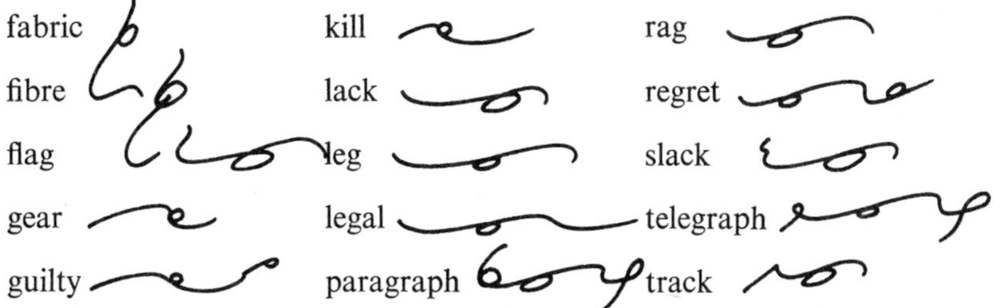

fabric	kill	rag
fibre	lack	regret
flag	leg	slack
gear	legal	telegraph
guilty	paragraph	track

39. *O* hook on its side

Before ***n***

alone	grown	owner
cone	honour	stone
donate	known	thereon
drawn	loan	thrown
flown	on	tone

Before ***m***

chrome	dome	homes
comb	home	roam

Before ***r***

abnormal	floor	narrower
core	horn	nor
corn	horses	normal
corner	ignore	or
course	lower	oral
door	moral	orange
drawer	mortgage	organ

origin

original

store

storm

story

torch

tore

torn

Tory

Before l

call

coal

collar

college

dollar

golf

hole

holiday

knowledge

recall

roller

small

stolen

whole

wholesale

Downward character preceding o

ball

bolt

bomb

bone

bore

born

borrow

borrowers

fall

fault

foam

follow

foreign

pole

policy

polish

politics

porch

salt

shown

sole

solicitor

solid

solve

sorrow

source

vault

39. Phrases

he calls

I call

on it

on its

on our

on sale

on the

on these

or more

40. *Th*

Over ***th***

death	smith	theme
faith	teeth	thicker
method	theatre	thin

Under ***th****—joined to* ***o***

author	clothing	though
both	growth	thought

Under ***th****—joined to* ***r***

earth	thorough	three
north	thread	throw

Under ***th****—joined to* ***l***

athlete	health	wealth
lathe	healthy	wealthy

Reading and Writing Practice

1

2

3

4

5

6

7

8

CHAPTER TWO

Lesson 7

50. Brief Forms

Dear Madam	must	were
Dear Sir	right	write
Dear Sirs	rights	year
desire	that	years
desires	them	you
hereto	to	your
market	too	yours
Mr	two	Yours truly

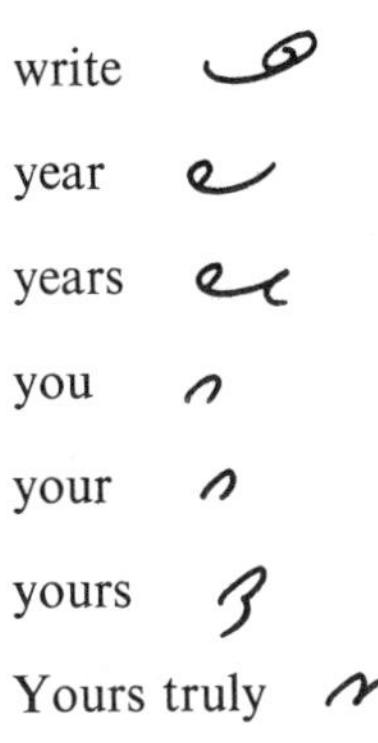

50. Phrases

he must	I must have	that must be
he must be	I must say	must have
he must have	must be	you must
I must	she must	you must be
I must be	she must be	you must have

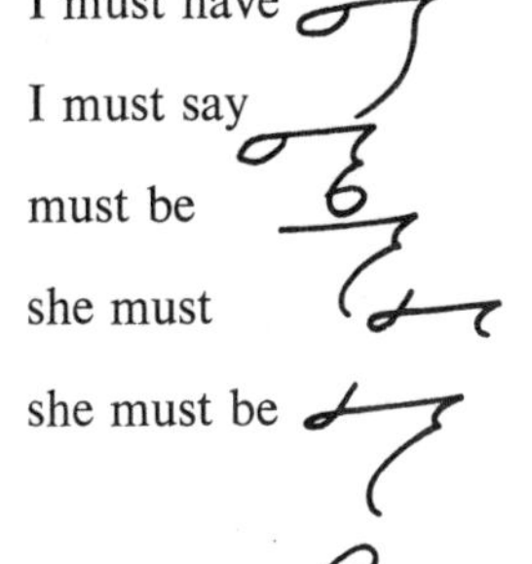

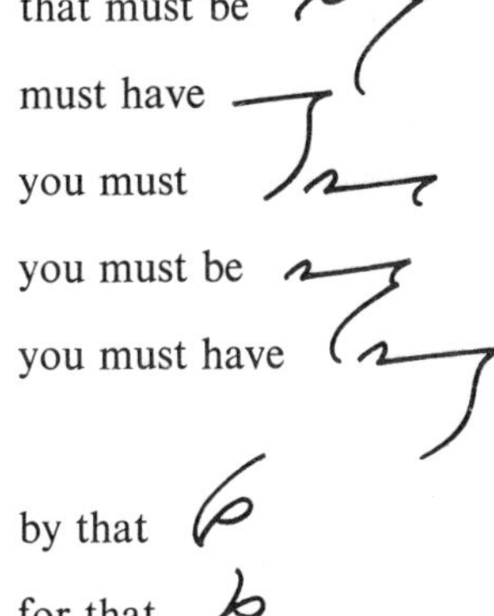

as that	at that	by that
ask that	before that	for that

hope that	that are	that may be
hope that the	that are not	that our
hoping that	that have	that the
if that is	that is	that their
in that	that is not	that there are
is that	that is the	that there is
is that the	that it	that these
of that	that it has	that will
on that	that it is	that will be
on that day	that its	that will not
realize that	that it will	that would
so that	that it will be	that would be
so that the	that may	with that

ask them	in them	to them
for them	of them	with them

as to	to care	to claim
as to that	to carry	to clean
as to the	to cash	to clear
to call	to catch	to climb
to cancel	to cause	to close

to gain	to its	to their
to get	to taste	to these
to give	to take	to tie
to go	to talk	to trade
to grow	to tell	to train
to his	to that	to travel
to it	to the	to try

as you	asking you	if you care
as you are	before you	if you could
as you can	by you	if you could not
as you go	can you	if you get
as you have	for you	if you go
as you know	have you	if you have
as you may	hope you will	if you have not
as you may have	give you	if you know
as you say	giving you	if you need
as you will	if you	if you see
as you will see	if you are	if you will
as you will not	if you are not	if you will be
as you would	if you can	if you will have
as you would be	if you can be	if you will see
ask you	if you cannot	if you would

if you would be
if you would have
in which you
in which you are
of you
reach you
serve you
serving you
to have you
to which you are
to you
which you
which you can
which you may
which you would
with you
you are
you are not
you can
you can be
you can have
you can get
you cannot

you cannot see
you can see
you can't
you could
you could be
you could have
you could not
you could see
you gave
you have
you have had
you have made
you have not
you have seen
you have the
you know
you made
you make
you may
you may be
you may have
you may not
you may not be

you might
you might be
you might have
you might not
you need
you need not
you say
you see
you shall have
you take
you will
you will be
you will have
you will not
you will not be
you will see
you would
you would be
you would have
you would not
you would not be
you wrote

as to your
as your
ask your
before your
by your

for your
have your
if your
of your
of yours

on your
to your
with your
your name
your needs

if it were

there were

were not

I write

I will write

write me

he desires
I desire

if you desire

you desire
My dear sir

51. Word-beginning *ex-*

example
exceed
exceeding
except
excess
excessive
exchange
exhibit

expedite
expense
expenses
expensive
expert
expire
expires
explain

explains
express
expressed
exterior
extra
extras
extreme
inexpensive

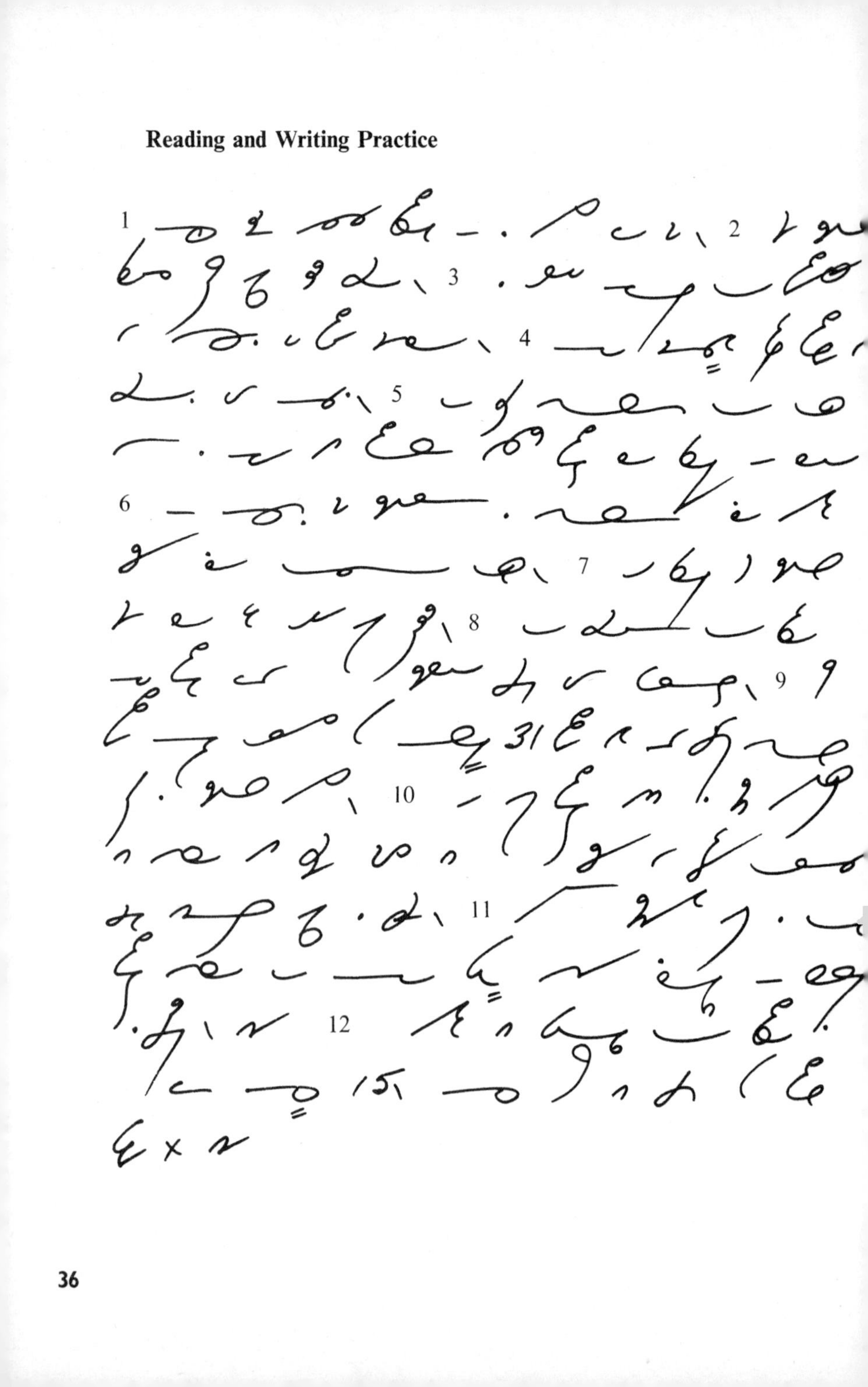

Reading and Writing Practice

Lesson 8

56. Word-ending *-tion*

action	expansion	precaution
application	expiration	preparation
authorization	expression	prescription
cancellation	fashion	prevention
caution	mission	protection
collision	motion	ration
co-operation	national	relation
collection	occasion	section
corporation	operation	sectional
election	option	selection
exception	physician	session
exemption	portion	taxation
exhibition	possession	vacation

56. Phrases

for collection

in relation

57. Word-endings *-cient, -ciency*

ancient	efficiency	inefficiency
efficient	inefficient	patient

58. Word-ending *-tial*

beneficial	essential	essentials

financial	officials	social
initial	partial	special

60. Past tense; ***-er, -or***

initialled	marketed	writer
desired	shipped	writers

Reading and Writing Practice

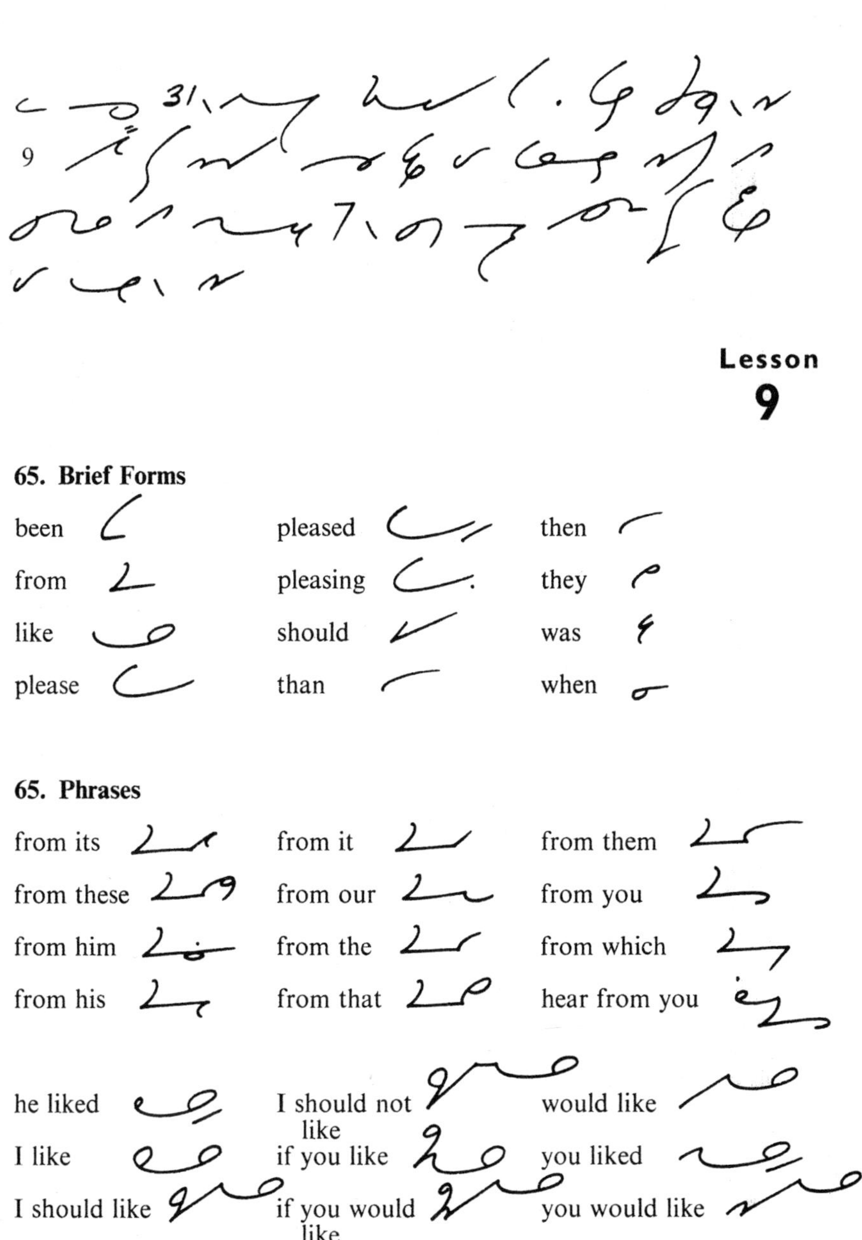

Lesson 9

65. Brief Forms

been	pleased	then
from	pleasing	they
like	should	was
please	than	when

65. Phrases

from its	from it	from them
from these	from our	from you
from him	from the	from which
from his	from that	hear from you
he liked	I should not like	would like
I like	if you like	you liked
I should like	if you would like	you would like

please be
please have
please see

please ship
please sign
please write

please write me
to please

he should
he should be
he should have
I should
I should be

I should have
I should say
should be
should have
should like

should not be
you should
you should be
you should have
you should not

less than
less than that

less than the
more than

since then
than the

as they
as they are
before they
if they
if they are
if they are not
if they can
if they would
if they would be

that they
that they are
that they will
they are
they are not
they can
they can be
they can have
they cannot

they can't
they could
they could not
they have
they may
they may be
they must
they will
they will be

they will have	they will see	they would buy
they will not	they would	they would not

when our	when the	when they
when that	when these	when they are

he was	that it was	was that
I was	that there was	was the
it was	there was	which was
it was the	was it	

66. *Been* in phrases

could have been	have not been	there has been
had been	having been	there have been

67. *Able* in phrases

be able	he will be able	shall be able
been able	he will not be able	to be able

68. Word-ending *-ly*

amply	calmly	deeply
badly	clearly	earlier
barely	closely	early
briefly	daily	excessively

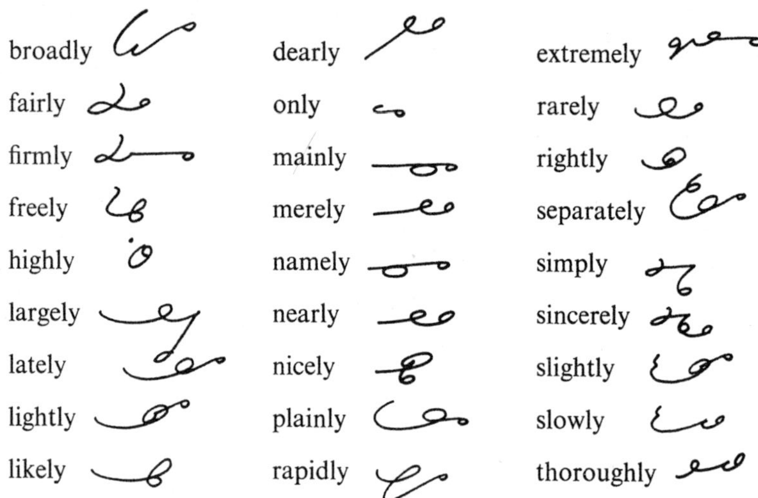

broadly	dearly	extremely
fairly	only	rarely
firmly	mainly	rightly
freely	merely	separately
highly	namely	simply
largely	nearly	sincerely
lately	nicely	slightly
lightly	plainly	slowly
likely	rapidly	thoroughly

69. Word-endings *-ily, -ally*

easily	financially	normally
especially	heartily	occasionally
essentially	heavily	originally
exceptionally	legally	principally
families	locally	readily
family	materially	specially
finally	nationally	totally

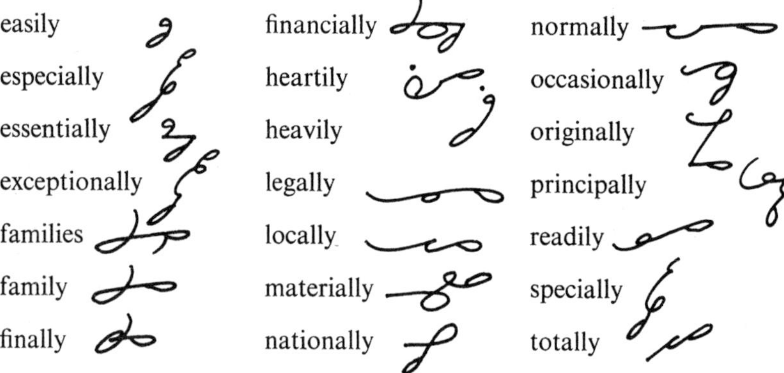

Reading and Writing Practice

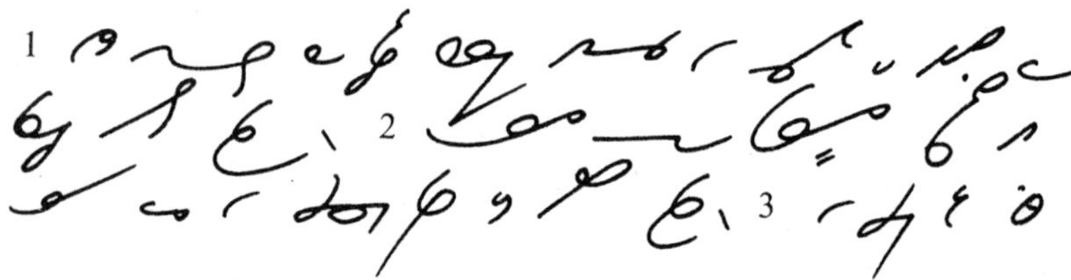

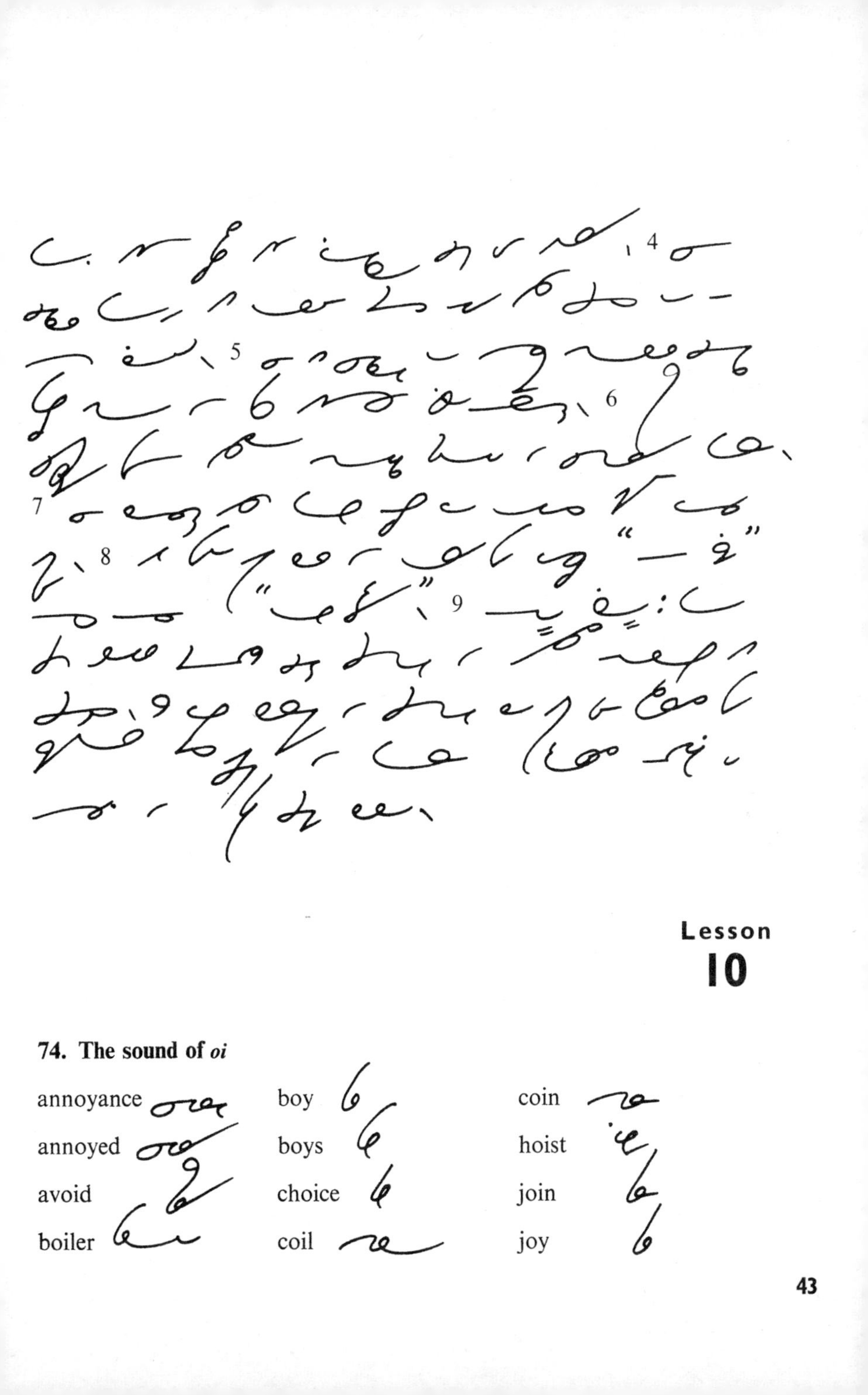

Lesson 10

74. The sound of *oi*

annoyance	boy	coin
annoyed	boys	hoist
avoid	choice	join
boiler	coil	joy

loyal poison toy
noise royal voice
oil soil void

75. Word-endings *-ure, -ture, -ual, -tual*

failure lecture pasture
feature literature picture
actual equal schedules
actually equally semi-annual

76. Omission of vowel in word-beginnings

re-

reason region resale
refine register research

be-

became begin below
because beginning behalf
began begins betray

de-

debit deliberate depot
delays deposits derive

des-, dis-

describe despite disbursed
description destroy disclose

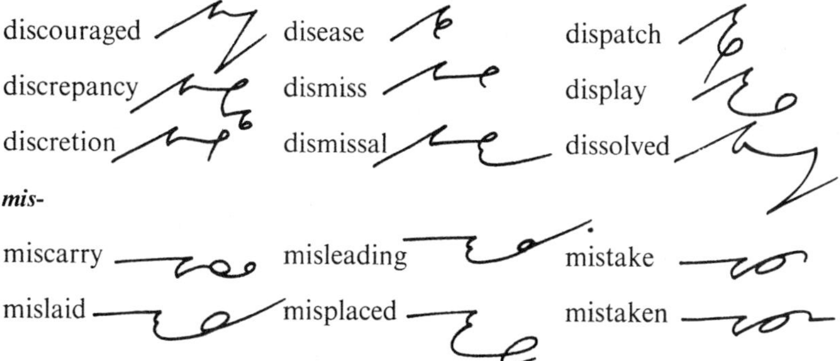

discouraged	disease	dispatch
discrepancy	dismiss	display
discretion	dismissal	dissolved

mis-

miscarry	misleading	mistake
mislaid	misplaced	mistaken

74-76. Phrases

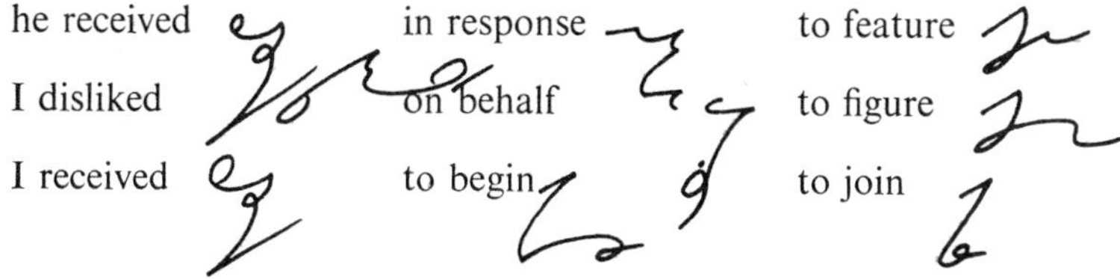

he received	in response	to feature
I disliked	on behalf	to figure
I received	to begin	to join

Reading and Writing Practice

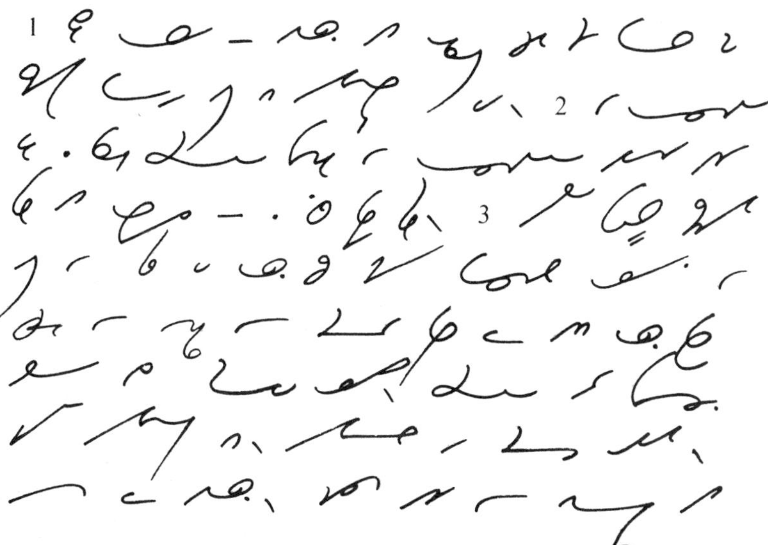

Lesson 11

81. Brief Forms

after

all

and

aside

besides

billing

bills

business

businesses

businesslike

decide

decided

decidedly

ended

hand

handle

most

mostly

Mrs

side

what

81. Phrases

after that
after them
after which
after the
after these

and are
and say
and they
and have
and see
and was
and his
and that
and which
and I am
and that is
and will
and is
and the
and will be
and our
and their
and will not

he decided
I decided
if you decide

what are
what is
what will
what has been
what is the
what will be

all right
for most
of all

82. Any vowel after the long *i*

appliance
diameter
science
bias
diet
trial
diagnosis
drier
via
dial
prior
violation

83. The dotted circle

appreciate	bacteria	obviate
appreciation	create	piano
area	creation	radiation
areas	depreciation	radiator
association	librarian	variation

84. Hook and circle vowels joined

drawee	poetry	rayon
poems	radio	snowy

Reading and Writing Practice

1

2

3

4

5

6

7

8

9

10

Lesson 12

88. ***Been* in phrases**

had not been	I have been	which have been
has been	it has been	would have been
has not been	should have been	you have been
have been	to have been	you have not been

89. ***Able* in phrases**

being able	he should be able	will be able
has been able	he would be able	you may be able
has not been able	I have not been able	you must be able
have been able	I shall be able	you should be able
have not been able	I shall not be able	you will be able
he may be able	I will be able	you would be able

90. Word-beginning *re-*

reappear	rechecked	reserved
readdress	refining	resources
reasons	repair	response
rebate	repeat	reveal
receipt	replace	reverse
receive	replied	revise
reception	reserve	revision

90. *E* written in *re-*

reclaim	regain	rename
redress	remake	retire

91. Word-beginning *de-*

decision	deposit	deserve
delay	depositor	design
delayed	depository	designer

91. *E* written in *de-*

declare	decline	degrade

92. Brief Forms

about	gladly	send
enclose	leaflet	thing
enclosed	let	think
enclosure	letter	thinking
glad	letters	thinks

this		work		worker	
very		worked		works	

92. Phrases

about it		about that		about these	
about its		about the		about this	
about my		about them		about which	

after this		in this		this man	
as this		in this case		this may	
at this		of this		this may be	
before this		on this		this means	
by this		on this side		this was	
for this		since this		this was the	
from this		that this		this will	
hope that this		that this is		this would	
if this		this can be		this would be	
if this is		this is		to this	
if this is not		this is not		when this	
if this is the		this is the		with this	

and let		as your letter		for your letter	

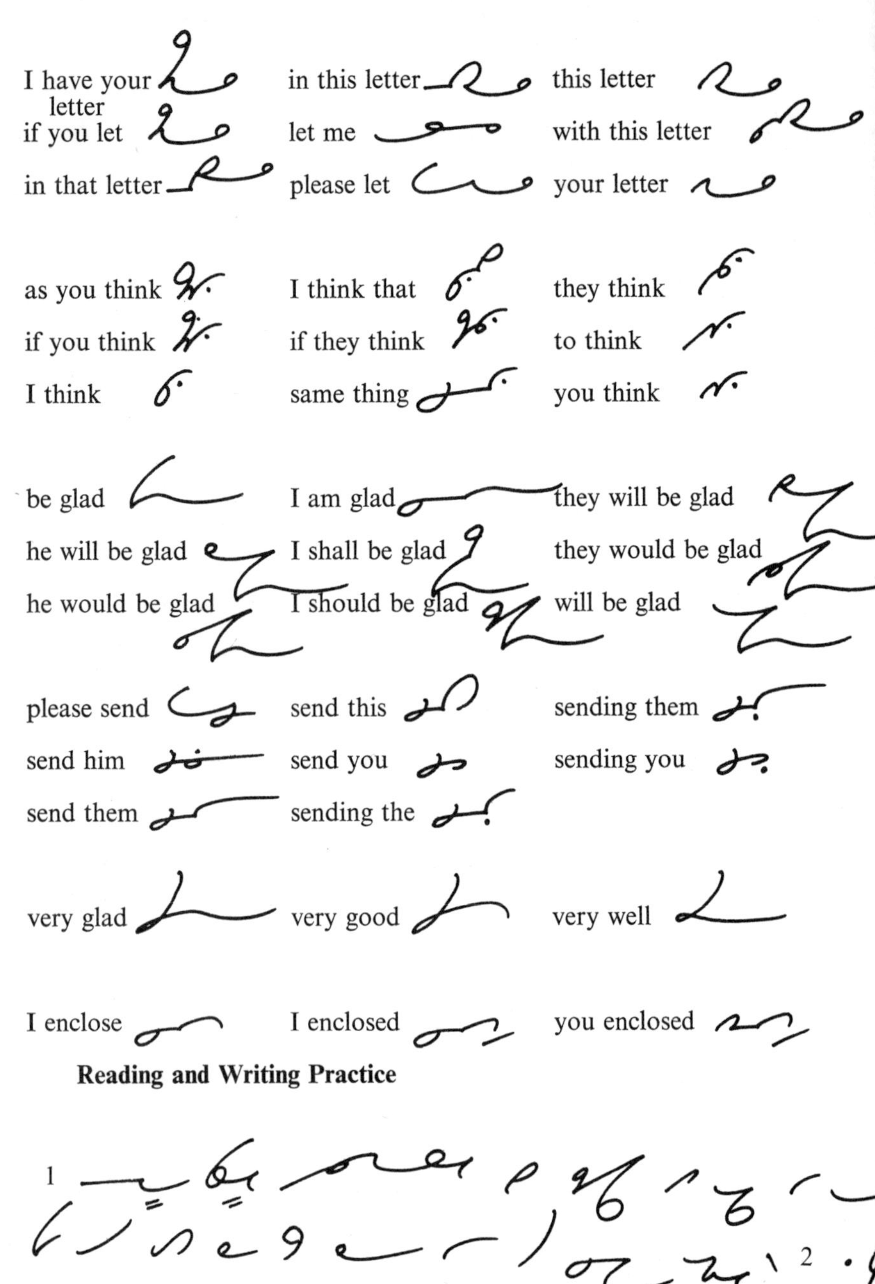

I have your letter ** in this letter ** this letter **

if you let ** let me ** with this letter **

in that letter ** please let ** your letter **

as you think ** I think that ** they think **

if you think ** if they think ** to think **

I think ** same thing ** you think **

be glad ** I am glad ** they will be glad **

he will be glad ** I shall be glad ** they would be glad **

he would be glad ** I should be glad ** will be glad **

please send ** send this ** sending them **

send him ** send you ** sending you **

send them ** sending the **

very glad ** very good ** very well **

I enclose ** I enclosed ** you enclosed **

Reading and Writing Practice

1 2

3

4

5

6

7

Lesson 13

CHAPTER THREE

100. The *oo* hook

u as in up

above	drug	rub
apparatus	duck	rubber
blood	dug	shovels
bud	dust	status
bulbs	hurry	stub
bulk	illustrate	stuff
butter	illustrations	suction
chorus	luck	suffer
colour	nothing	sufficient
couple	oven	thus
cups	plug	tough
cut	plus	truck
disastrous	production	trust
discussion	reduction	up
does	reproduction	us
dozen	rough	utterly

o͝o as in book

book
booked
booklet
bush
cook
cooker

foot
full
fully
hook
look
looked

pull
push
shook
stood
sugar
took

oo as in who

accrued
blue
booth
boots
cool
coupon
crude
do
drew
exclude
exclusive
food
fruit
glued
grew

group
grouped
jewel
jewellers
jewellery
juvenile
loose
lose
pool
poor
prune
roof
room
root
route

routine
rule
school
screw
shoe
spoon
through
tool
tooth
tour
true
who
whom
whose
withdrew

100. Phrases

do it	I do not like	you do not
do not	I do not see	you do not like
do not let	I do not think	you do not say
do so	if you do	does not
do this	if you do not	he does
do you	if you do not like	he does not
do you think	they do	that does not
I do	they do not	this does not
I do not	you do	which does

who are	who have made	who might have
who are not	who is	who might like
who can	who knows	who must
who can be	who like	who should
who cannot	who made	who should be
who could	who make	who takes
who desire	who makes	who taught
who do not	who may	who thinks
who go	who may be	who will
who have	who might	who will be
who have had	who might be	who would

who would be	who would like	for whom
who would have	who would not	to whom

above the	I trust	to choose
check up	send us	to cut
he discussed	sending us	to push
he looks	through its	to shoot
he took	through that	to trust
I discussed	through the	up to
I look	through them	up to its
I looked	through these	up to the
I took	to book	up to this

Reading and Writing Practice

1

2

3

4

5

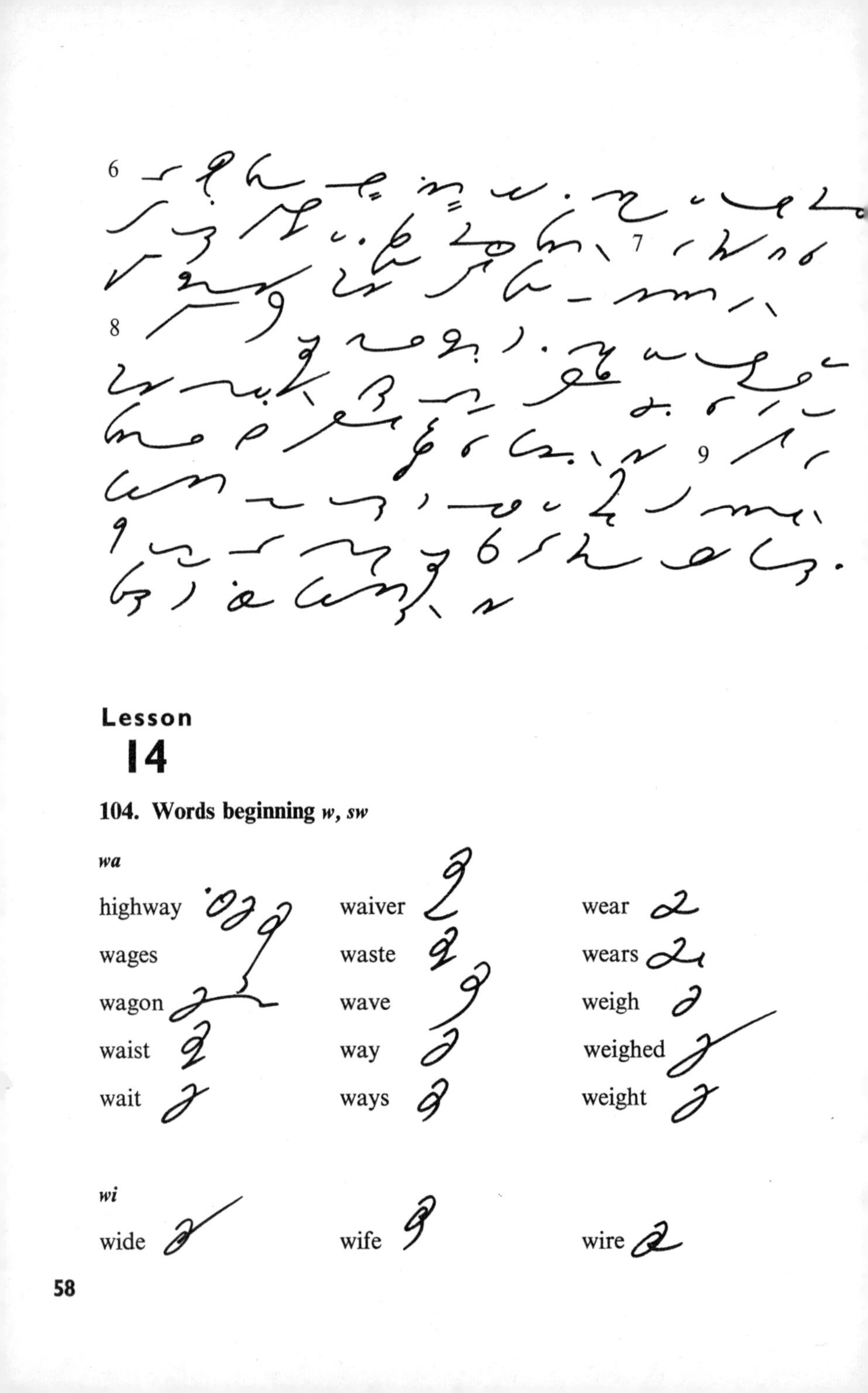

6

7

8

9

Lesson 14

104. Words beginning *w, sw*

wa

highway	waiver	wear
wages	waste	wears
wagon	wave	weigh
waist	way	weighed
wait	ways	weight

wi

wide	wife	wire

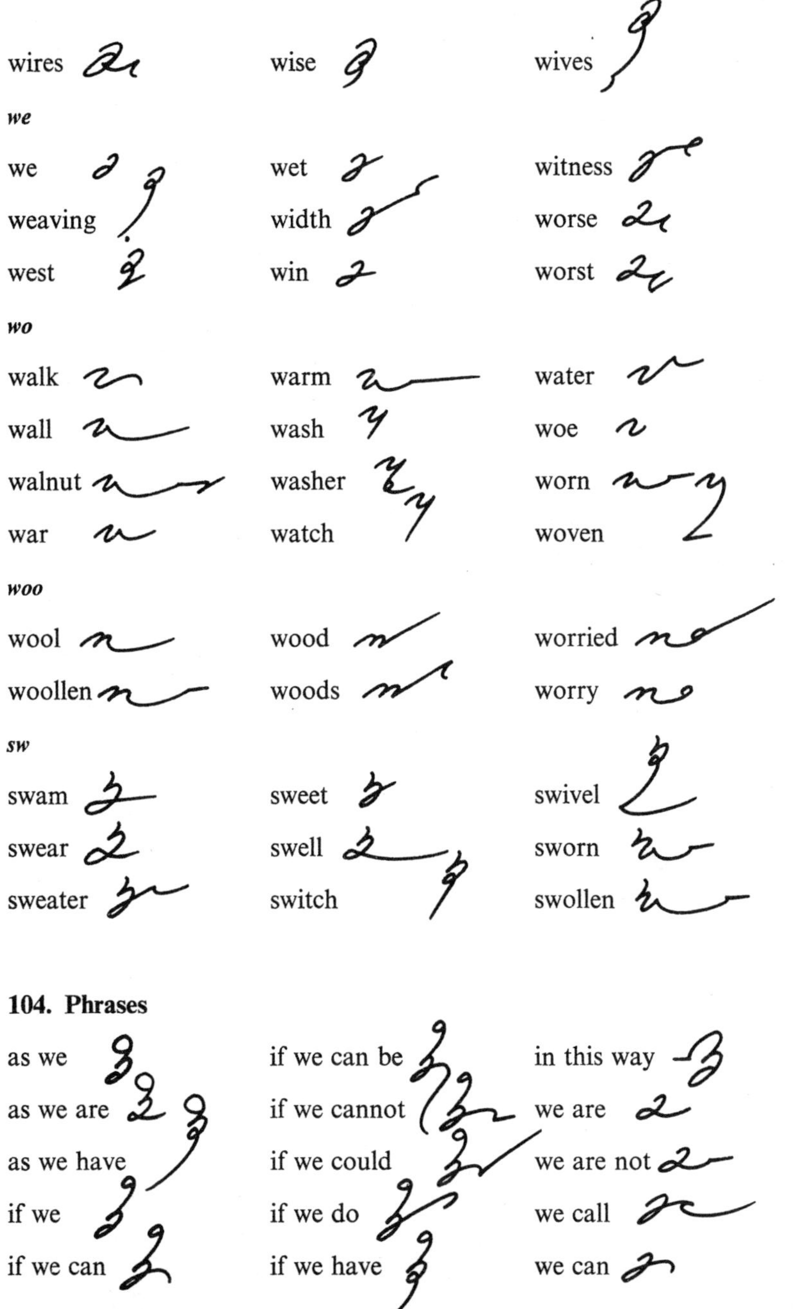

wires	wise	wives

we

we	wet	witness
weaving	width	worse
west	win	worst

wo

walk	warm	water
wall	wash	woe
walnut	washer	worn
war	watch	woven

woo

wool	wood	worried
woollen	woods	worry

sw

swam	sweet	swivel
swear	swell	sworn
sweater	switch	swollen

104. Phrases

as we	if we can be	in this way
as we are	if we cannot	we are
as we have	if we could	we are not
if we	if we do	we call
if we can	if we have	we can

we can be
we can have
we can make
we cannot
we cannot be
we can say
we can't
we could
we could be
we could have
we could not
we decide
we decided
we desire
we do
we do not
we do not say
we do not see
we do not think
we enclose
we feel
we get
we give

we have
we have been
we have been able
we have decided
we have given
we have had
we have made
we have not
we have not been
we have not been able
we have not had
we have your letter
we know
we made
we make
we may
we may be
we may be able
we may have
we mean
we might
we might be able
we must

we must have
we need
we note
we notice
we shall
we shall be
we shall be able
we shall be glad
we shall have
we shall mail
we shall make
we shall need
we shall not
we shall not be able
we shall see
we should
we should be
we should have
we should like
we should not
we should not like
we should say
we take

we think	we will have	we would be glad
we think that	we will not	we would have
we thought	we will not be	we would like
we took	we will pay	we would not
we tried	we will see	we would not be able
we trust	we will send	we would say
we try	we will ship	we wrote
we will	we would	which we
we will be	we would be	which we are

105. Words beginning *wh*

whale	wheel	whip
wheat	while	white

106. Word-ending *-ther*

another	father	mother
bother	feather	neither
bothered	gather	rather
brother	other	together
either	others	weather
farther	leather	whether

106. Phrases

each other	other side	to gather
he gathered	other than	we gathered
I gathered	to bother	whether or not

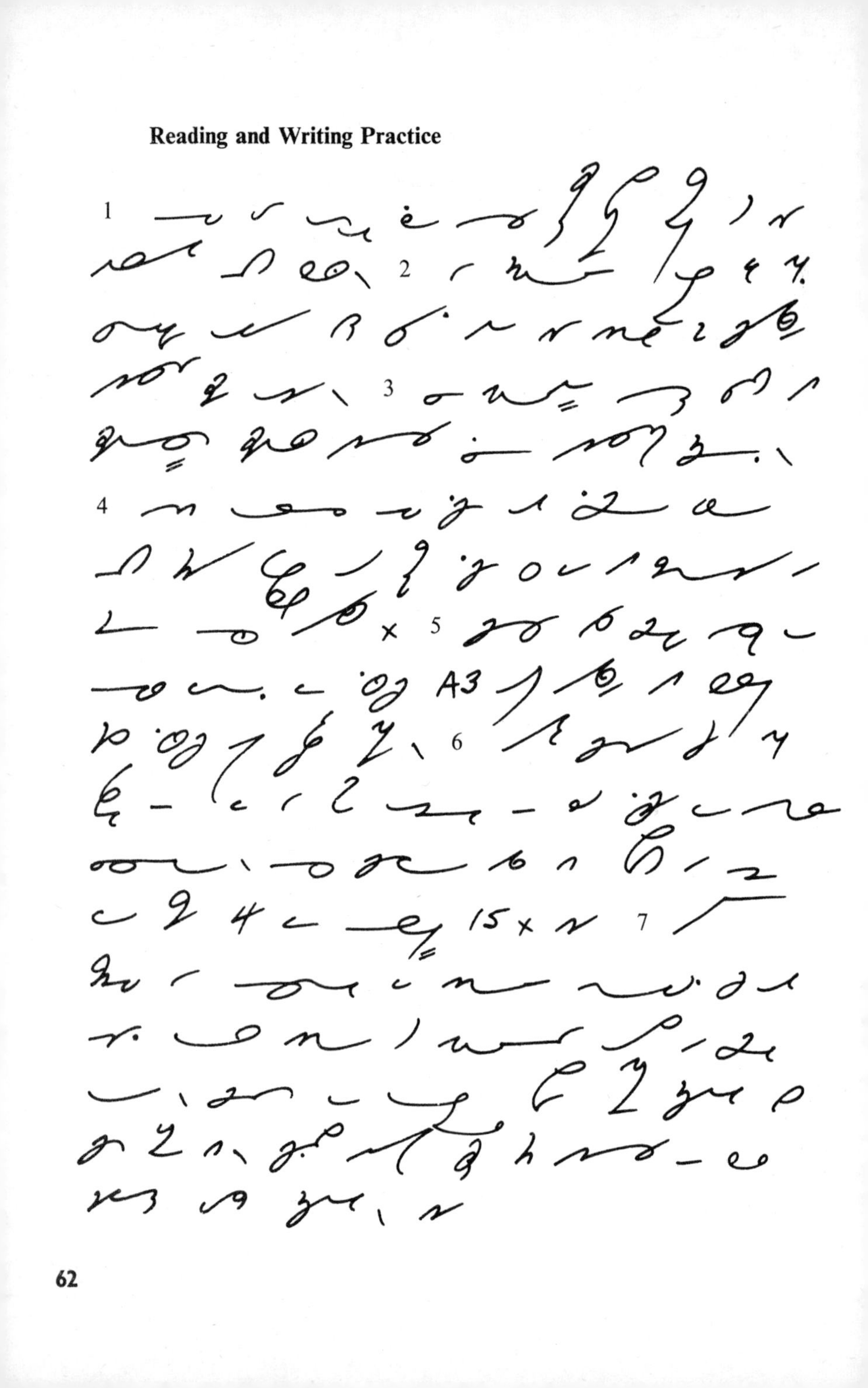

Reading and Writing Practice

1

2

3

4

5

6

7

Lesson 15

110. Brief Forms

belief
believe
believer
believes
deliver
delivered
deliveries
dissatisfaction
dissatisfied
doctor
during
necessarily
necessary
next
return
returned
satisfaction
satisfactorily
satisfactory
satisfied
satisfy
worth
worthy
yet

110. Phrases

as necessary
as yet
has not yet
has not yet been
have not yet
have not yet been
he returns
I believe
I do not believe
I have not yet
I returned
if necessary
in return
is not yet
next meeting
next year
next year's
of work
please return
to believe
we have not yet

111. The sound of *w* within a word

Broadway
doorway
dwelling
equip
equipped
liquid
queen
query
quick

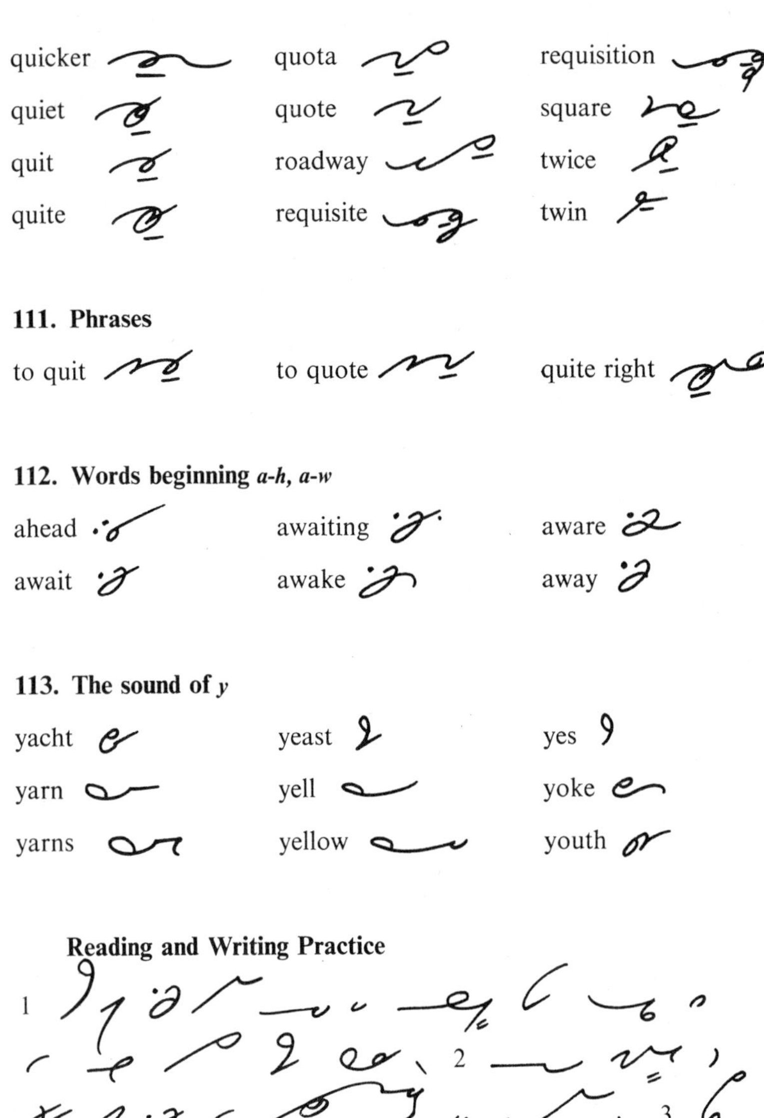

quicker　quota　requisition

quiet　quote　square

quit　roadway　twice

quite　requisite　twin

111. Phrases

to quit　to quote　quite right

112. Words beginning *a-h, a-w*

ahead　awaiting　aware

await　awake　away

113. The sound of *y*

yacht　yeast　yes

yarn　yell　yoke

yarns　yellow　youth

Reading and Writing Practice

1 2 3 4

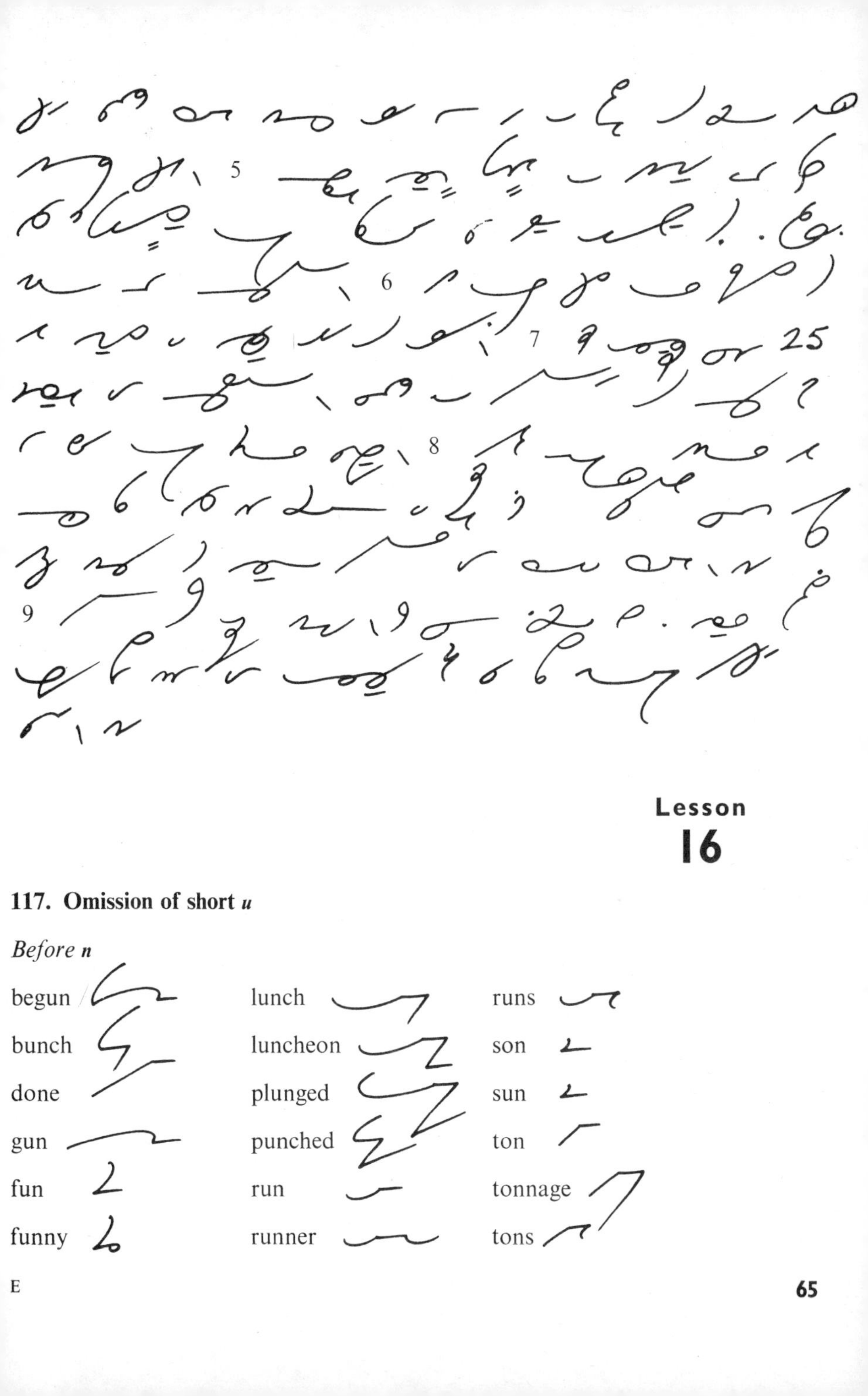

Lesson 16

117. Omission of short *u*

Before n

begun	lunch	runs
bunch	luncheon	son
done	plunged	sun
gun	punched	ton
fun	run	tonnage
funny	runner	tons

Before m

become	lumber	something
bumper	lump	sum
column	plumbing	summary
come	pump	summer
drum	some	welcome

Before a downstroke

brush	crushed	rush
brushed	flush	rushed
budget	judge	rushing
clutch	much	touch

117. Phrases

as much	I come	to become
be done	much more	to come
can be done	much more than	to judge
cannot be done	must be done	too much
can't be done	please rush	very much
could be done	should be done	we have done
has come	so much	who comes
has done	something like	who have done
have done	they come	will be done
I have done	to be done	would be done

118. Stroke for *ng*

angle	ring	strong
bring	shingle	strongly
finger	sing	sung
hanger	single	swing
hung	song	swung
king	spring	tongue
language	strength	wrong
length	string	young

119. Stroke for *ngk*

anchor	crank	link
ankle	drinking	pink
bank	frank	sanction
banker	frankly	shrinkage
bankruptcy	functions	sink
banquet	handkerchief	tank
blank	ink	trunk
blanket	junction	uncle

Reading and Writing Practice

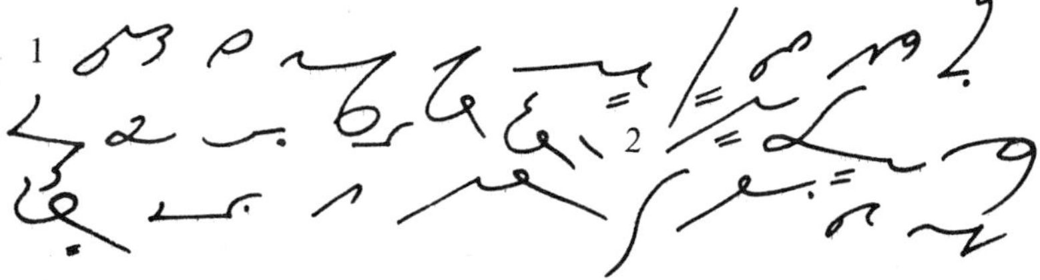

Lesson 17

123. Brief Forms

accompanied	among	book-keeping
along	belong	companies

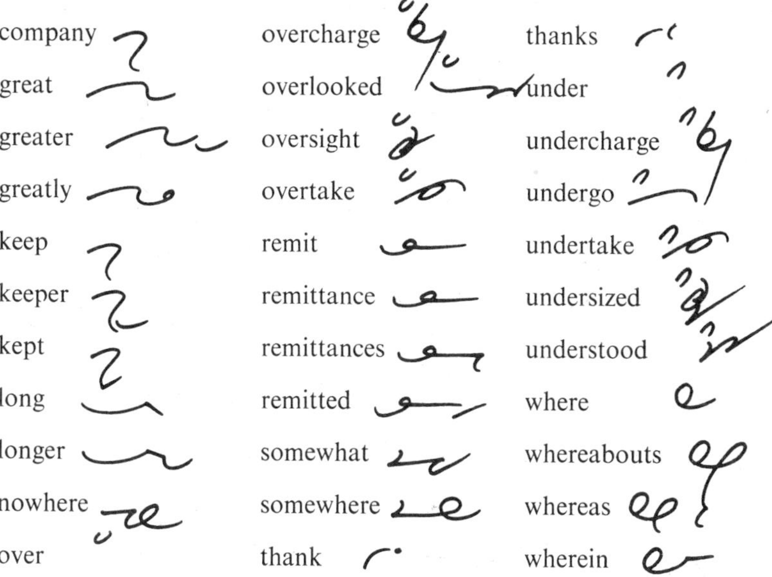

company	overcharge	thanks
great	overlooked	under
greater	oversight	undercharge
greatly	overtake	undergo
keep	remit	undertake
keeper	remittance	undersized
kept	remittances	understood
long	remitted	where
longer	somewhat	whereabouts
nowhere	somewhere	whereas
over	thank	wherein

123. Phrases

along the	thank you for this
along this	thank you for your
among the	thank you for your letter
among them	this company
among these	to keep
as long	to thank you for
if you keep	to thank you for your
so long	we thank you for
thank you	we thank you for the
thank you for	we thank you for this
thank you for the	we thank you for your

124. Stroke for *rd*

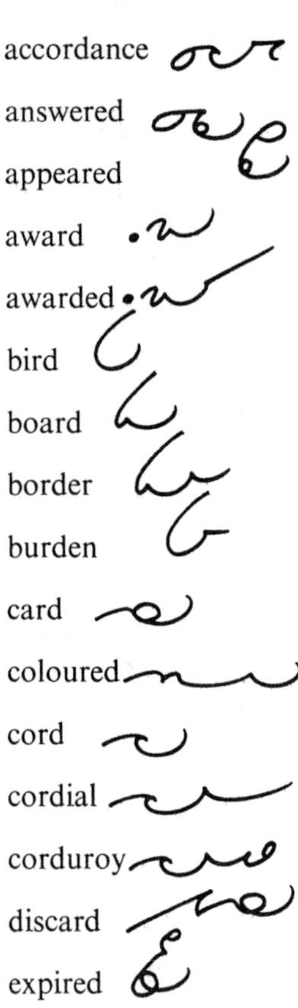
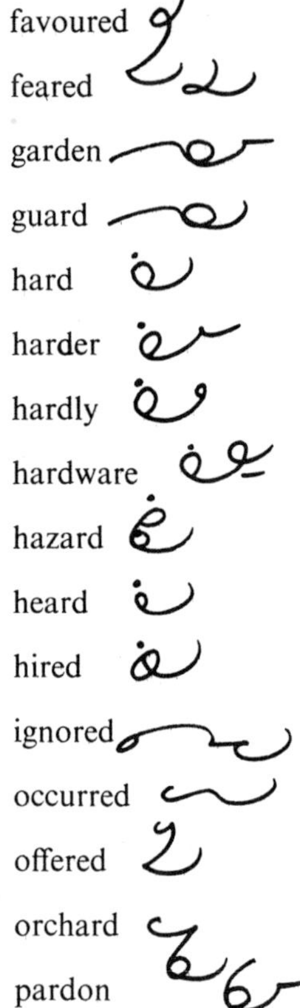
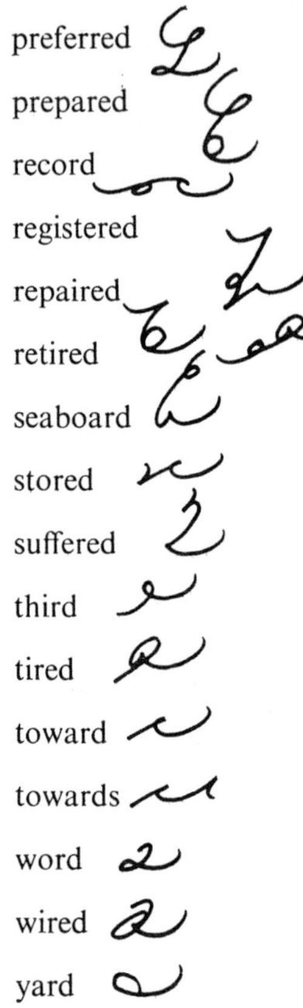

accordance	favoured	preferred
answered	feared	prepared
appeared	garden	record
award	guard	registered
awarded	hard	repaired
bird	harder	retired
board	hardly	seaboard
border	hardware	stored
burden	hazard	suffered
card	heard	third
coloured	hired	tired
cord	ignored	toward
cordial	occurred	towards
corduroy	offered	word
discard	orchard	wired
expired	pardon	yard

125. Stroke for *ld*

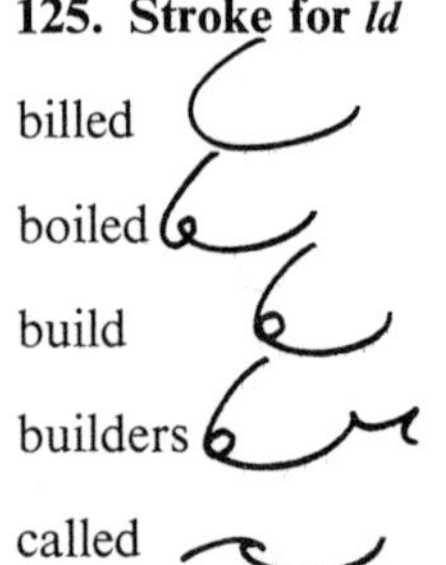
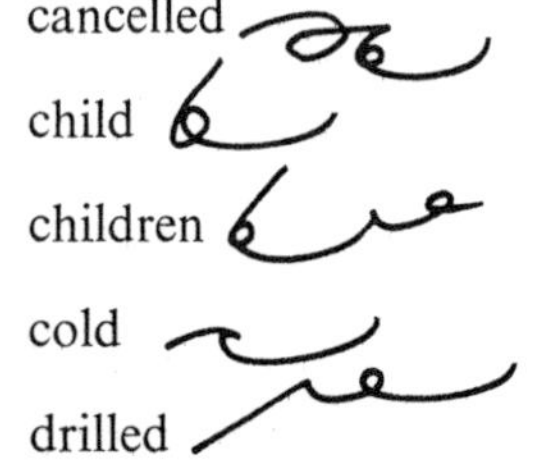
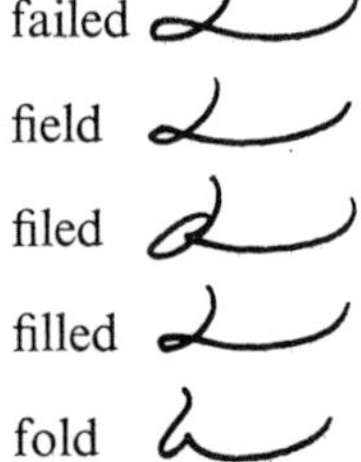

billed	cancelled	failed
boiled	child	field
build	children	filed
builders	cold	filled
called	drilled	fold

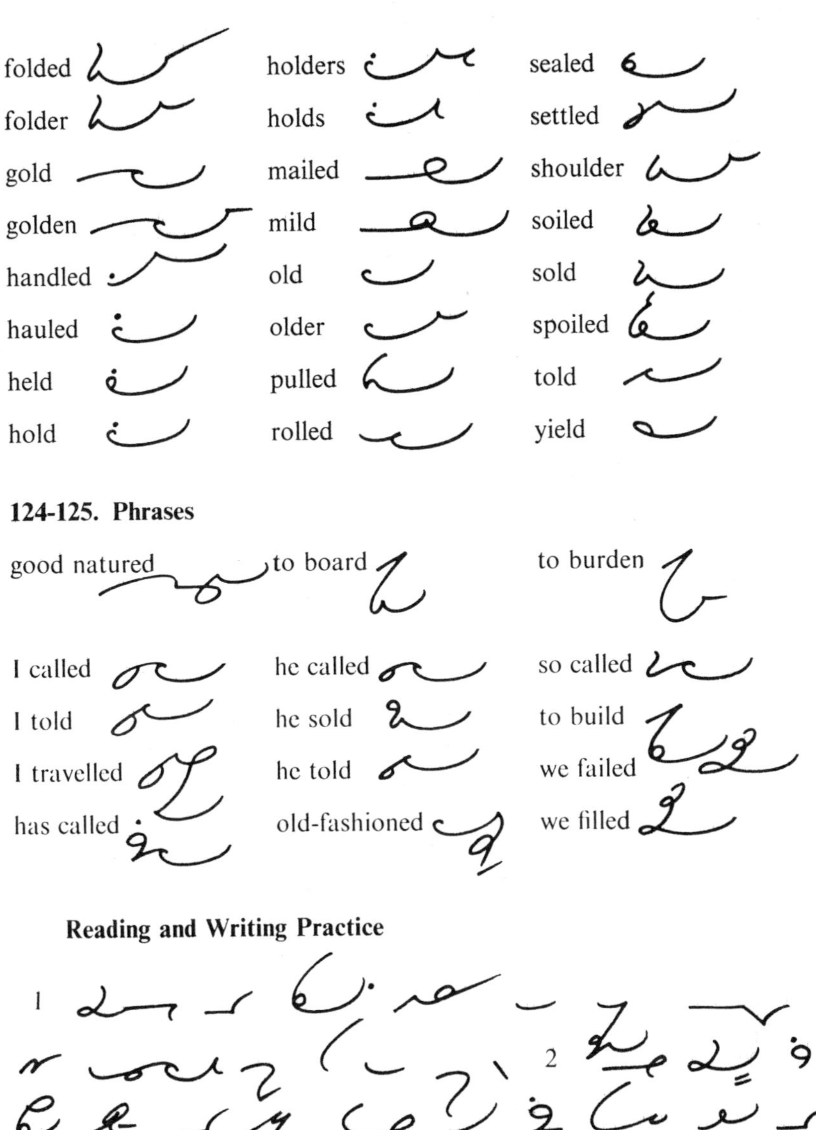

folded	holders	sealed
folder	holds	settled
gold	mailed	shoulder
golden	mild	soiled
handled	old	sold
hauled	older	spoiled
held	pulled	told
hold	rolled	yield

124-125. Phrases

good natured	to board	to burden
I called	he called	so called
I told	he sold	to build
I travelled	he told	we failed
has called	old-fashioned	we filled

Reading and Writing Practice

Lesson 18

129. ***Oo* hook on its side**

annum	move	noon
bonus	mud	nut
enormous	muslin	remove
famous	none	smooth

130. Word-endings *-ure, -ual*

-ure

fixtures	natural	procure
mature	naturally	secure
moisture	pictures	signature

-ual

actually	annually	gradually
annual	gradual	virtually

After a downstroke

assurance	measure	surely
assured	measures	treasurer
assures	pleasures	treasury
juries	pressure	casually
jury	sure	visual

130. Phrases

be sure	feeling sure	to be sure
being sure	I am sure	we are sure
can be sure	if you are sure	you can be sure
feel sure	please be sure	you may be sure

131. *S* with *f, v, k, g, oo*; and *p, b, r, l*

Comma s with f, v

arrives	fast	gives
facilitate	fiscal	graphs

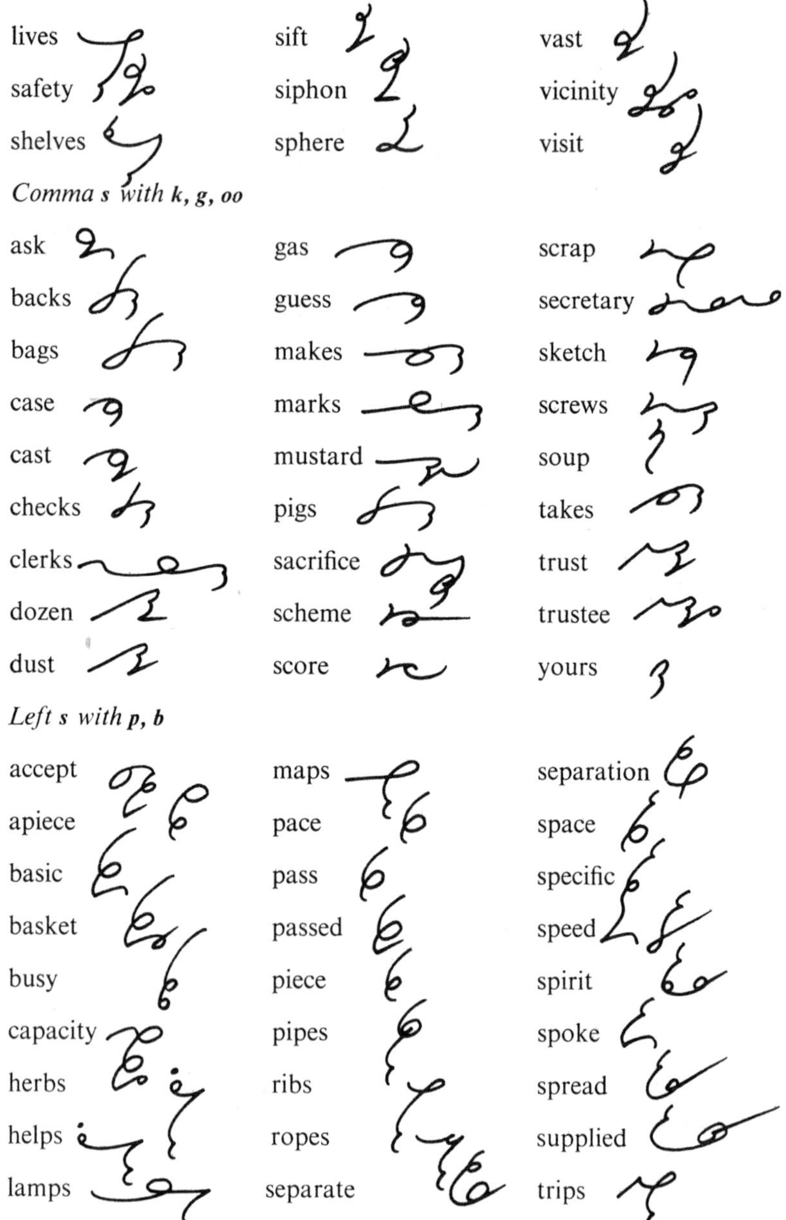

lives
safety
shelves
sift
siphon
sphere
vast
vicinity
visit

Comma s with **k, g, oo**

ask
backs
bags
case
cast
checks
clerks
dozen
dust
gas
guess
makes
marks
mustard
pigs
sacrifice
scheme
score
scrap
secretary
sketch
screws
soup
takes
trust
trustee
yours

Left s with **p, b**

accept
apiece
basic
basket
busy
capacity
herbs
helps
lamps
maps
pace
pass
passed
piece
pipes
ribs
ropes
separate
separation
space
specific
speed
spirit
spoke
spread
supplied
trips

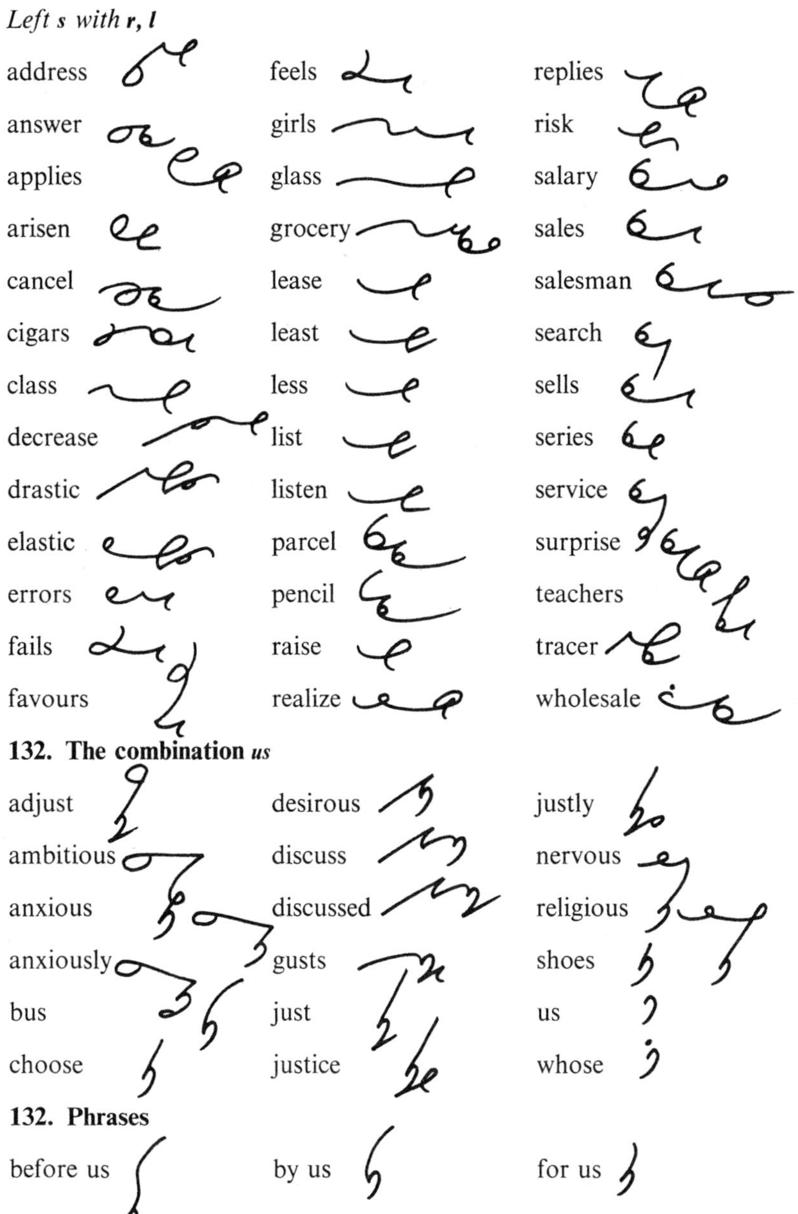

Left s with **r, l**

address	feels	replies
answer	girls	risk
applies	glass	salary
arisen	grocery	sales
cancel	lease	salesman
cigars	least	search
class	less	sells
decrease	list	series
drastic	listen	service
elastic	parcel	surprise
errors	pencil	teachers
fails	raise	tracer
favours	realize	wholesale

132. The combination ***us***

adjust	desirous	justly
ambitious	discuss	nervous
anxious	discussed	religious
anxiously	gusts	shoes
bus	just	us
choose	justice	whose

132. Phrases

before us	by us	for us

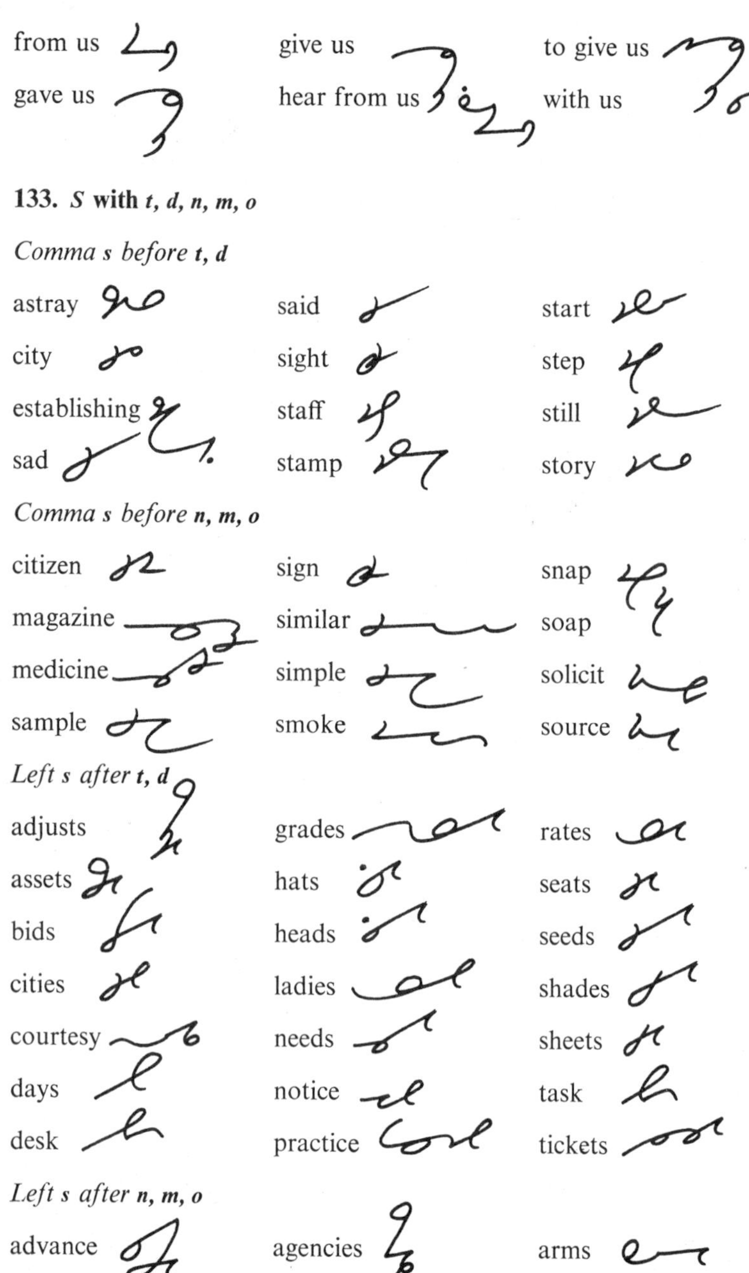

from us gave us give us hear from us to give us with us

133. ***S* with *t, d, n, m, o***

Comma s before t, d

astray said start city sight step establishing staff still sad stamp story

Comma s before n, m, o

citizen sign snap magazine similar soap medicine simple solicit sample smoke source

Left s after t, d

adjusts grades rates assets hats seats bids heads seeds cities ladies shades courtesy needs sheets days notice task desk practice tickets

Left s after n, m, o

advance agencies arms

balance
chance
chosen
Christmas
claims
close
coast
currency
farms
fellows
finance
firms

frames
glance
gross
happens
homes
illness
knows
lessons
lines
machines
means
miss

names
pins
plans
post
principal
rose
seems
shows
sickness
since
sincerely
vacancies

134. Comma *s* before and after *sh, ch, j*

ashes
branches
bridges
brushes
changes
charges
cheese

chest
dishes
ditches
edges
hinges
matches
messages

packages
pages
reaches
sessions
siege
washes
wrenches

135. *S*, or *s* and *th* with circle vowel

as
has

say
see

seethe
these

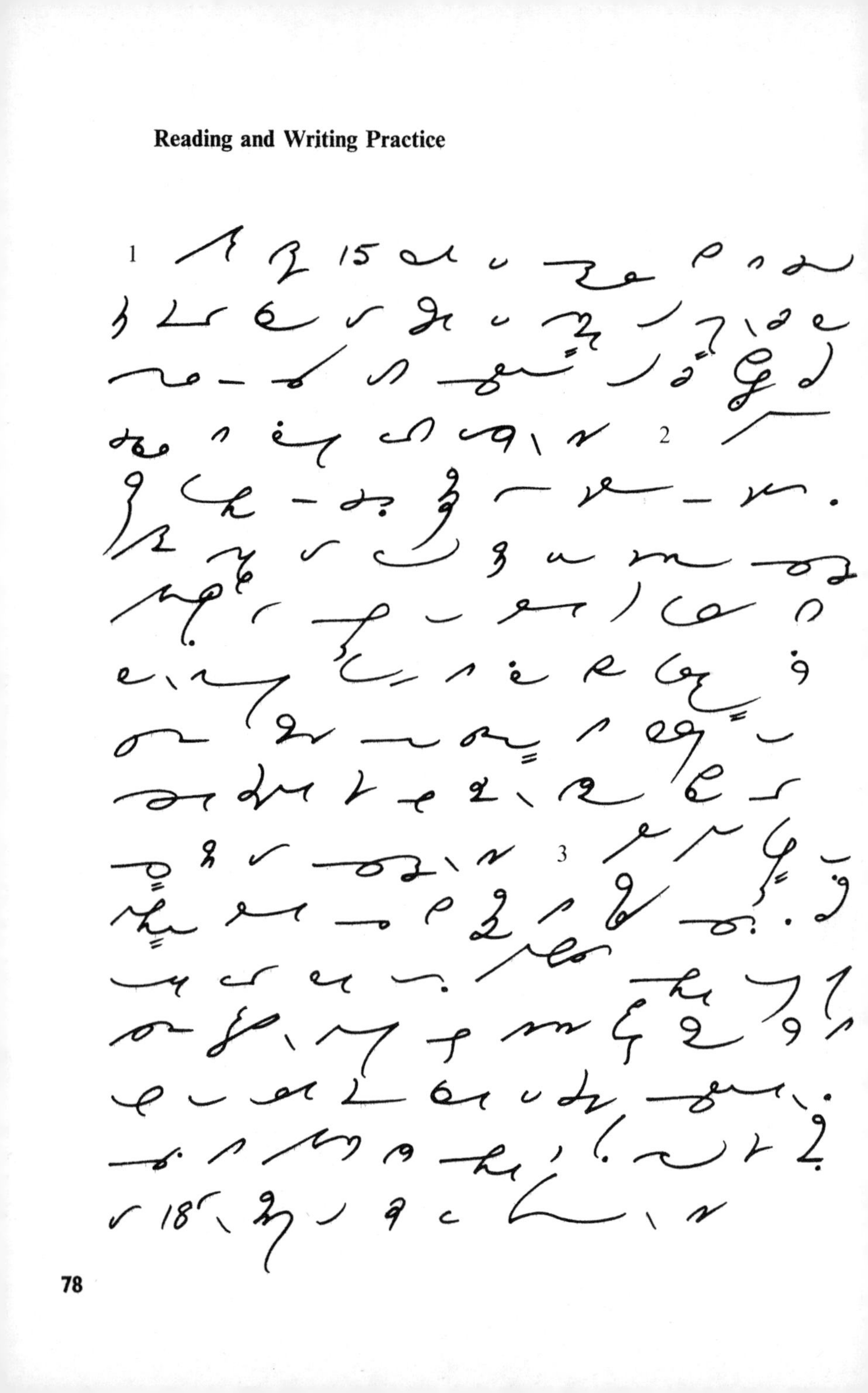

Reading and Writing Practice

1

2

3

CHAPTER FOUR

Lesson 19

142. The sound of *u* as in *cube*

acute
argue
bureau
cubic
cure
dispute
few

fewer
fuel
peculiar
pure
rescue
review
reviews

tube
unique
unit
unite
utilization
view
views

143. The sound of *ow*

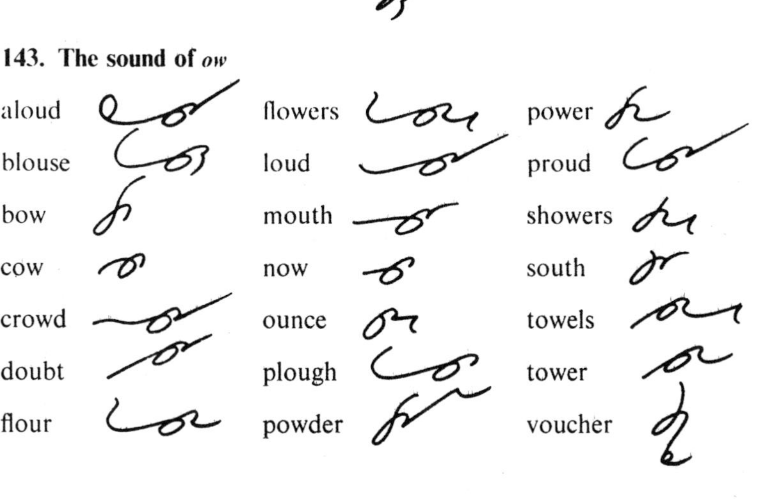

aloud
blouse
bow
cow
crowd
doubt
flour

flowers
loud
mouth
now
ounce
plough
powder

power
proud
showers
south
towels
tower
voucher

142-143. Phrases

in view
few days

I doubt
in our power

is now
no doubt

right now	we are now	we doubt

144. Brief Forms

ever	one	used
every	out	users
how	outline	uses
importance	outside	whatever
important	someone	whenever
matter	soon	wherever
matters	sooner	whichever
no-one	those	without
once	use	won

144. Phrases

about those	for one	one thing
along those	for one thing	one way
among those	from those	one year
and those	for those	only one
as those	how much	that those
at those	in this matter	these matters
by those	in those	this one
each one	of those	to those
ever had	one-half	very important
ever ready	on this matter	when those
ever since	once more	with those

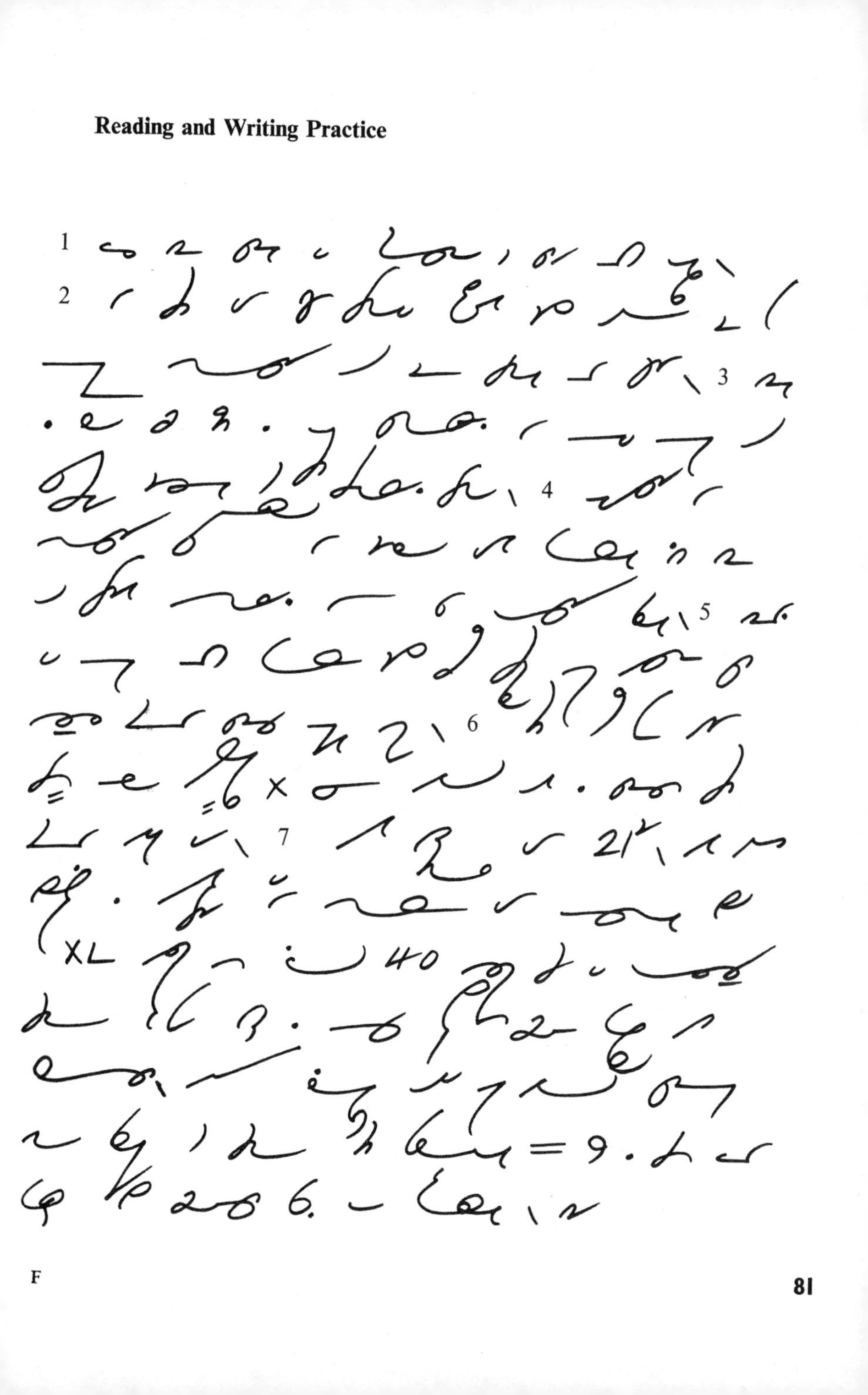

Reading and Writing Practice

1

2

3

4

5

6

7

Lesson 20

148. Brief Forms

always	suggest	weak
any	suggested	week
anyone	suggestion	weekly
anything	unable	wish
gone	unusually	wished
several	usual	world

148. Phrases

always be	for any one	if anything
any more	for any other	if you wish
any one	for anything	of any
any other	has gone	one week
any others	have gone	several days
business world	I wish	several other
for any	if any	several others

149. Blended consonants *ted*

accepted	adopted	benefited
adapted	appreciated	co-operated
adjusted	asserted	created
admitted	awaited	delighted

depleted
deposited
doubted
executed
excited
exhibited
fitted
hesitated
homestead
illustrated
lifted
limited
liquidated

listed
noted
omitted
operated
pasted
posted
quoted
rated
related
repeated
repeatedly
routed
separated

solicited
started
steadily
steady
studied
studies
study
today
treated
united
visited
waited
wasted

150. Blended consonants *ded, det, dit*

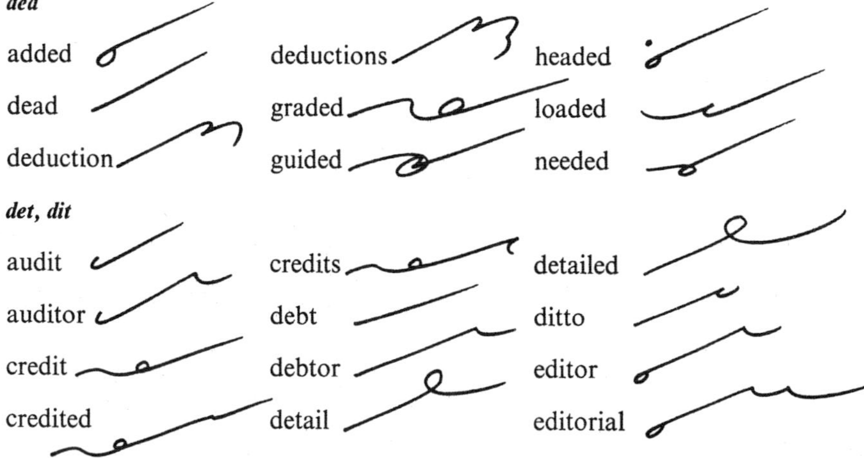

ded

added
dead
deduction

deductions
graded
guided

headed
loaded
needed

det, dit

audit
auditor
credit
credited

credits
debt
debtor
detail

detailed
ditto
editor
editorial

149-150. Phrases

he needed
I doubted
I needed
I noted
we needed
we noted

151. Blended consonants *men, mem*

cement
immensely
many
meant
member
memo
memorial
memory
men
mental
mentioned
salesmen
tremendous
women
workmen

151. Phrases

as many
he mentioned
how many
I mention
I mentioned
many other
many others
so many
these men
to mention
we mentioned
you mentioned

152. Blended consonants *min, mon,* etc.

administer
aluminium
eliminate
examine
examined
examiners
harmony
human
lemon
manage
managed
managers
manner
manual
maximum
mineral
miniature
minimum
ministry
minute
money

month	prominence	romance
monthly	remain	summons
nominal	remained	woman

152. Phrases

each month	few months	next month
every minute	I remain	several months
every month	in this manner	this month
few minutes	in this month's	we remain

Reading and Writing Practice

1

2

3

4

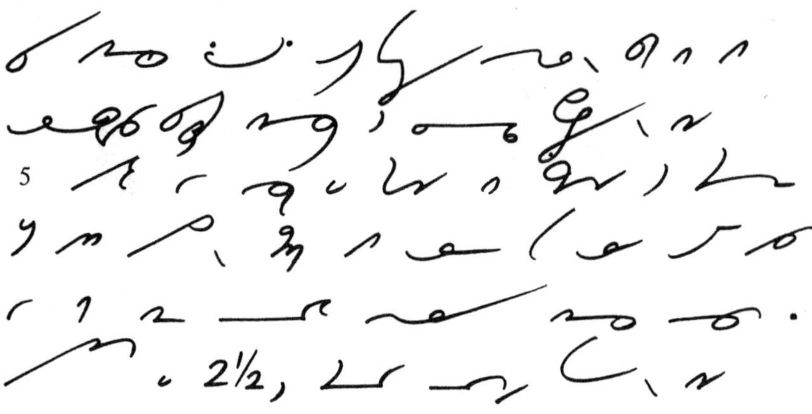

Lesson 21

156. Blended consonants *nd*

assigned
band
behind
beyond
bind
binder
bindery
blunder
bond
bonded
brand
burned

calendar
candy
canned
cleaned
cylinder
earned
explained
designed
fastened
find
friend
friendly

fund
gained
grand
grind
island
joined
kind
kindly
kindness
land
lands
learned

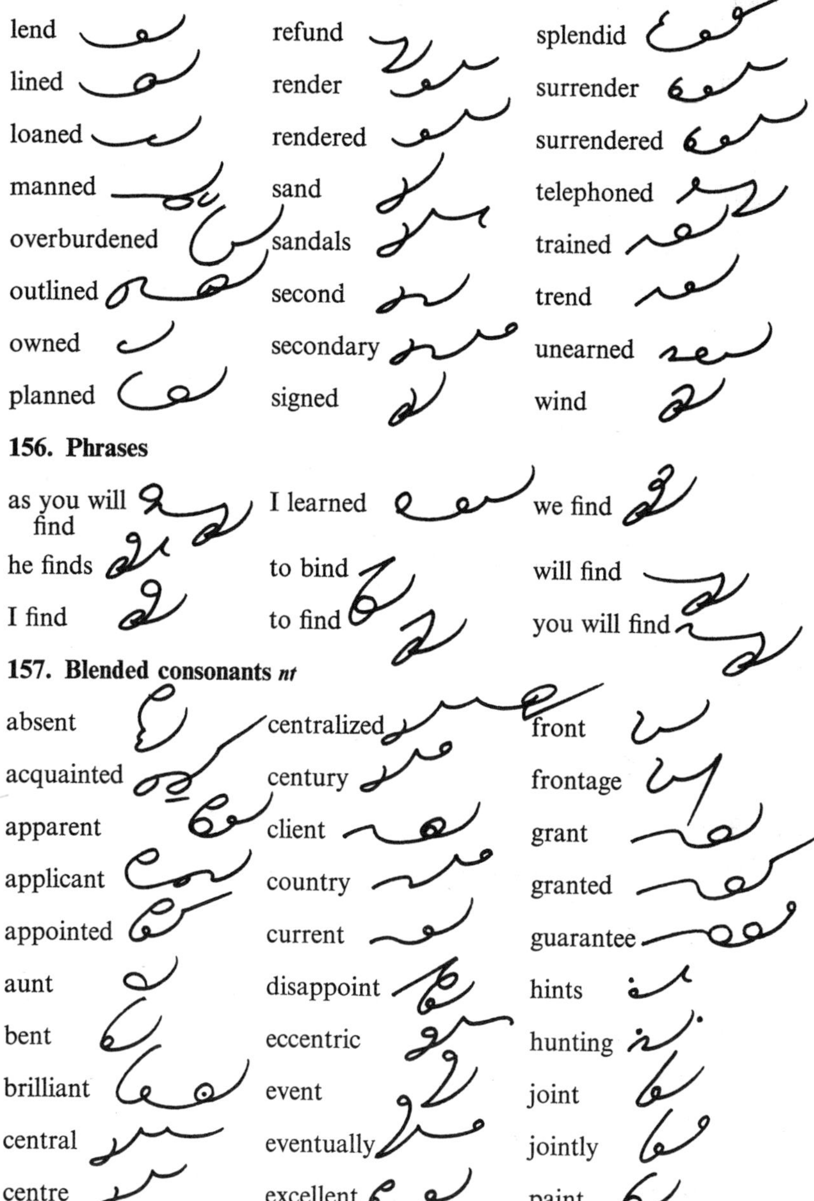

lend
lined
loaned
manned
overburdened
outlined
owned
planned

refund
render
rendered
sand
sandals
second
secondary
signed

splendid
surrender
surrendered
telephoned
trained
trend
unearned
wind

156. Phrases

as you will find
he finds
I find

I learned
to bind
to find

we find
will find
you will find

157. Blended consonants *nt*

absent
acquainted
apparent
applicant
appointed
aunt
bent
brilliant
central
centre

centralized
century
client
country
current
disappoint
eccentric
event
eventually
excellent

front
frontage
grant
granted
guarantee
hints
hunting
joint
jointly
paint

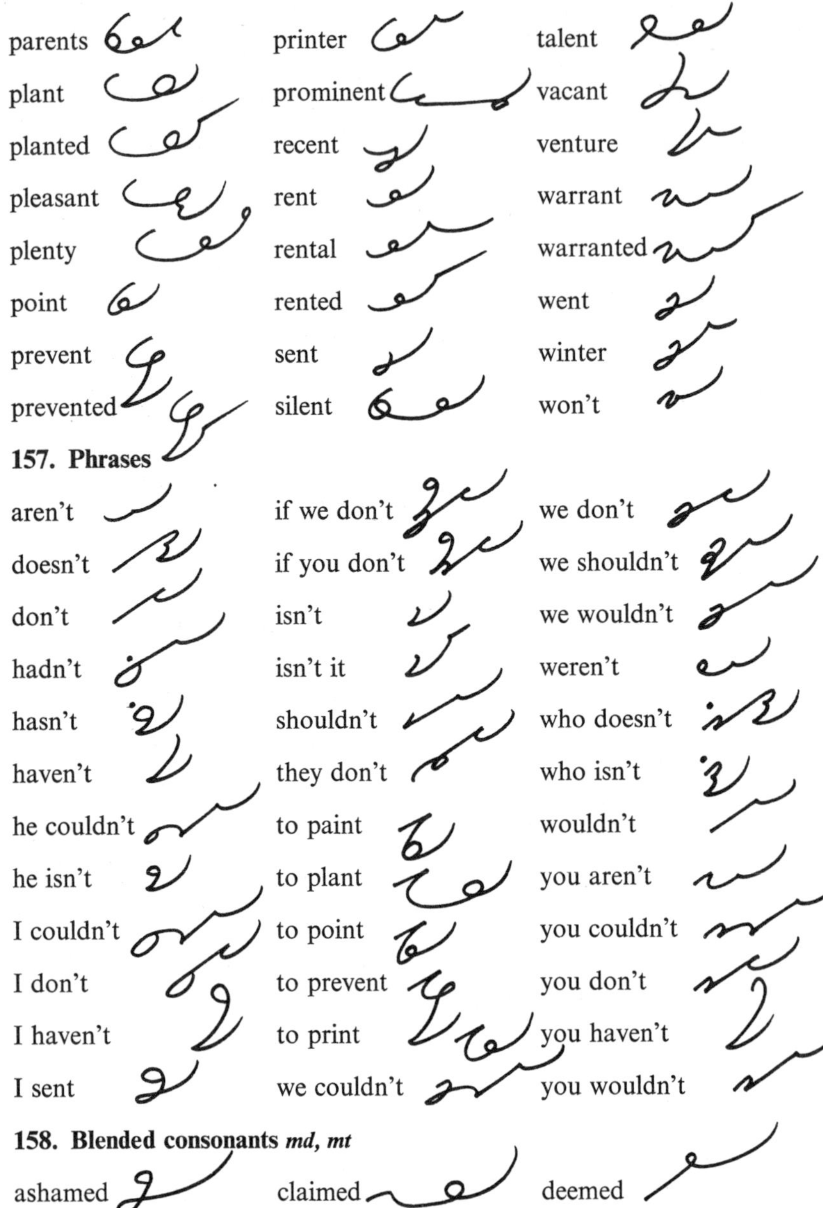

parents
plant
planted
pleasant
plenty
point
prevent
prevented

printer
prominent
recent
rent
rental
rented
sent
silent

talent
vacant
venture
warrant
warranted
went
winter
won't

157. Phrases

aren't
doesn't
don't
hadn't
hasn't
haven't
he couldn't
he isn't
I couldn't
I don't
I haven't
I sent

if we don't
if you don't
isn't
isn't it
shouldn't
they don't
to paint
to plant
to point
to prevent
to print
we couldn't

we don't
we shouldn't
we wouldn't
weren't
who doesn't
who isn't
wouldn't
you aren't
you couldn't
you don't
you haven't
you wouldn't

158. Blended consonants *md, mt*

ashamed
claimed
deemed

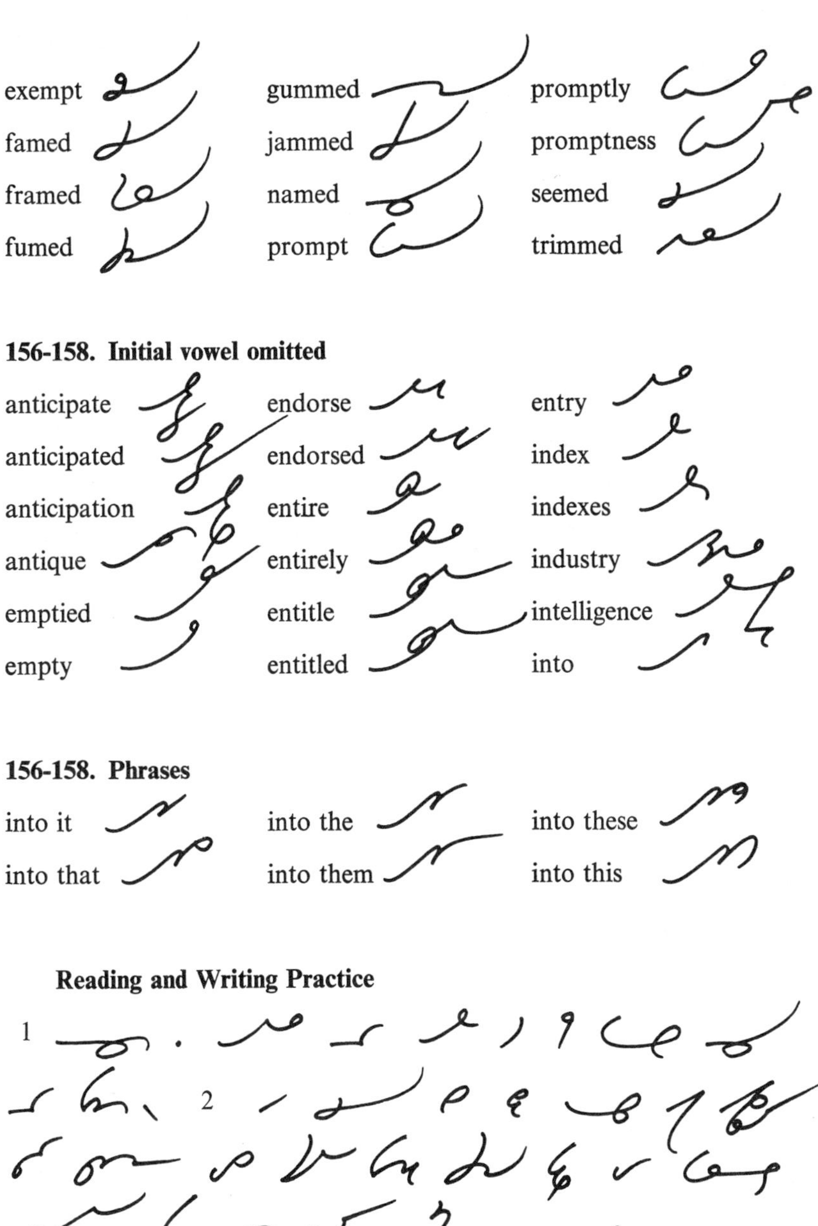

exempt
famed
framed
fumed
gummed
jammed
named
prompt
promptly
promptness
seemed
trimmed

156-158. Initial vowel omitted

anticipate
anticipated
anticipation
antique
emptied
empty
endorse
endorsed
entire
entirely
entitle
entitled
entry
index
indexes
industry
intelligence
into

156-158. Phrases

into it
into that
into the
into them
into these
into this

Reading and Writing Practice

Lesson 22

162. Brief forms

big	general	office
bigger	generalize	offices
date	generally	officers
dated	got	opportunity
dates	individual	want
did	morning	wanted

162. Phrases

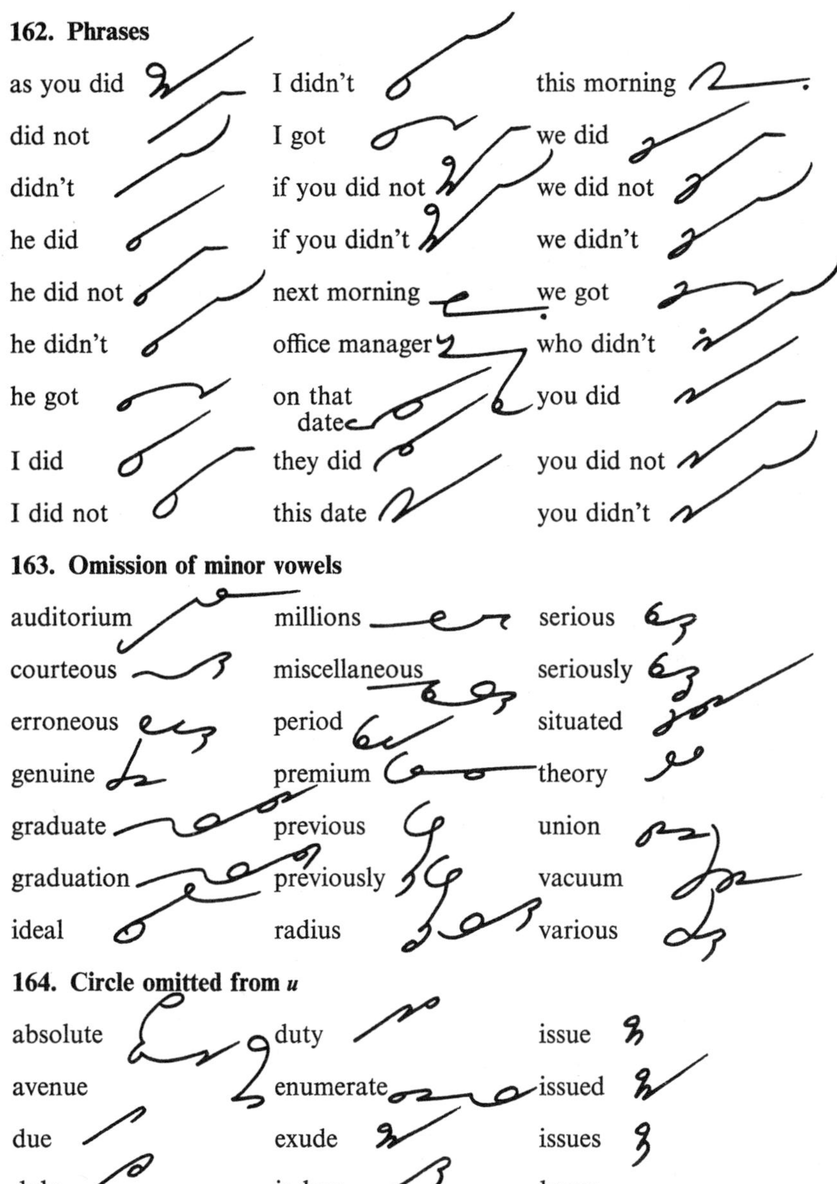

as you did
did not
didn't
he did
he did not
he didn't
he got
I did
I did not
I didn't
I got
if you did not
if you didn't
next morning
office manager
on that date
they did
this date
this morning
we did
we did not
we didn't
we got
who didn't
you did
you did not
you didn't

163. Omission of minor vowels

auditorium
courteous
erroneous
genuine
graduate
graduation
ideal
millions
miscellaneous
period
premium
previous
previously
radius
serious
seriously
situated
theory
union
vacuum
various

164. Circle omitted from *u*

absolute
avenue
due
duly
duty
enumerate
exude
induce
issue
issued
issues
knew

lieu
manufacture
manufactured
manufacturer
manuscript
music
mutual
mutually
new

newer
news
numerous
overdue
produce
produced
producers
produces
reduce

reduced
reduces
renew
renewal
renewed
revenue
strenuous
suited
volume

164. Phrases

he knew
I knew

in lieu
to produce

we knew
you knew

165. Days of the week

Sunday
Monday
Tuesday

Wednesday
Thursday

Friday
Saturday

165. Phrases

Friday morning
Friday night
Tuesday morning

Wednesday morning
Thursday morning
Saturday morning

166. Months of the year

January
February

March
April

May
June

July | September | November
August | October | December

Reading and Writing Practice

1

2

3

4

5

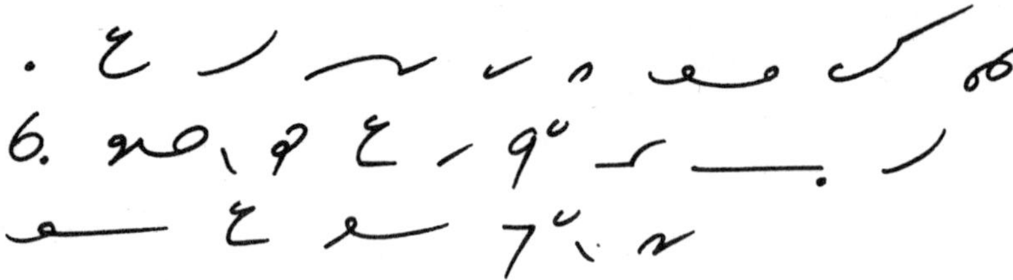

Lesson 23

170. Omission of *ow*

around
account
accountant
accounted
background
brown
council
counsel

count
counted
counter
counting
county
crown
discount
discounted

down
found
foundry
ground
round
sound
surrounding
town

moun

amount
amounted

amounting
amounts

mount
mounted

171. Omission of *ow* between *n-n*

announce

noun

renown

170-171. Phrases

he found
I found

on account
to count

we count
we found

172. Word-beginnings *per-, pur-*

per-

per	permit	personally
percentage	permitted	persons
perforated	perpetual	personnel
perforation	perplexing	persuade
perhaps	person	persuaded
permanent	personal	persuasion

pur-

purloin	pursuant	pursued
purple	pursue	pursuit

173. Word-beginning *pro-*

approach	probate	promise
approached	problem	promised
appropriate	procedure	promises
appropriation	proceed	promissory
approval	process	promote
approve	processes	promotion
approved	profess	proof
approximate	professional	proper
approximately	professor	properly
apron	profit	proportion
fireproof	prohibit	proportionate

proprietor	prove	provide
prosper	proved	provided
prosperous	proven	provision

172-173. Phrases

per cent	to permit	to promote
per hour	to persuade	to prove
per month	to proceed	to provide

174. Word-ending *-ment*

adjustment	elements	momentary
agreement	endorsement	monument
allotment	equipment	movement
announcement	establishment	non-payment
appointment	experiment	ornamental
arrangement	experimental	ornamented
assessment	experimented	payment
assignment	fundamental	replacement
basement	garment	settlement
casement	inducement	shipment
disagreement	judgment	supplement
document	management	supplemental
documentary	measurement	supplementary
elementary	moment	treatment

174. Phrases

few moments in payments on payment

175. Word-ending *-ble*

acceptable
adaptable
adjustable
advisable
agreeable
applicable
appreciable
available
cable
capable
desirable

disagreeable
double
eligible
equitable
favourably
feasible
flexible
inadvisable
liable
payable
possible

possibly
profitable
reasonably
reliable
responsible
saleable
suitable
table
trouble
troublesome
unaccountable

Reading and Writing Practice

1

2

3

Lesson 24

180. Word-ending *-ship*

fellowship	membership	scholarship
hardship	ownership	steamship
kinship	relationship	township

181. Word-endings *-cle, -cal*

analytical	article	chemical

chemicals	medical	practically
critical	musical	radical
geographical	periodical	statistical
historical	periodically	surgical
logical	physical	technical
mechanical	political	typical
mechanically	practical	typographical

182. Word-endings *-self, -selves*

herself	myself	themselves
himself	oneself	yourself
itself	ourselves	yourselves

182. Phrases

for itself	for themselves	in itself
for myself	for yourself	of ourselves
for ourselves	for yourselves	with themselves

183. Word-beginning *after-*

afterm̄ath   afternoon   afterthought

Reading and Writing Practice

1

2

3

4

5

6

7

8

CHAPTER FIVE

Lesson 25

191. Brief Forms

enable	progressive	speaks
order	property	street
ordered	purpose	streets
orders	purposes	such
progress	speak	upon

191. Phrases

for the purpose	on such	upon this
in order that	to speak	upon us
in such	upon such	upon which
no such	upon the	upon you
of such	upon them	with such

192. Blended consonants *gend, gent*

agenda	genteel	intelligent
cogent	gentle	intelligently
diligent	gentleman	urgent
diligently	gently	urgently

193. Blended consonants *pend, pent*

appendix	carpenter	depend

dependable	expended	respond
depended	expenditure	respondent
dependent	happened	spend
depends	opened	spent
expend	pending	suspend

194. Blended consonants *def, dif*

defence	defiance	differ
defer	definite	difference
deferred	defy	different

195. Blended consonants *dev, div*

device	development	divert
devise	develops	diverted
devised	devote	divide
develop	devoted	divided
developed	diversion	division

196. Blended consonants *tive, tif*

appreciative	executive	negative
authoritative	initiative	positive
co-operative	locomotive	positively
creative	motive	relative
descriptive	native	scientific

192-196. Phrases

to spend	to defeat	to devote

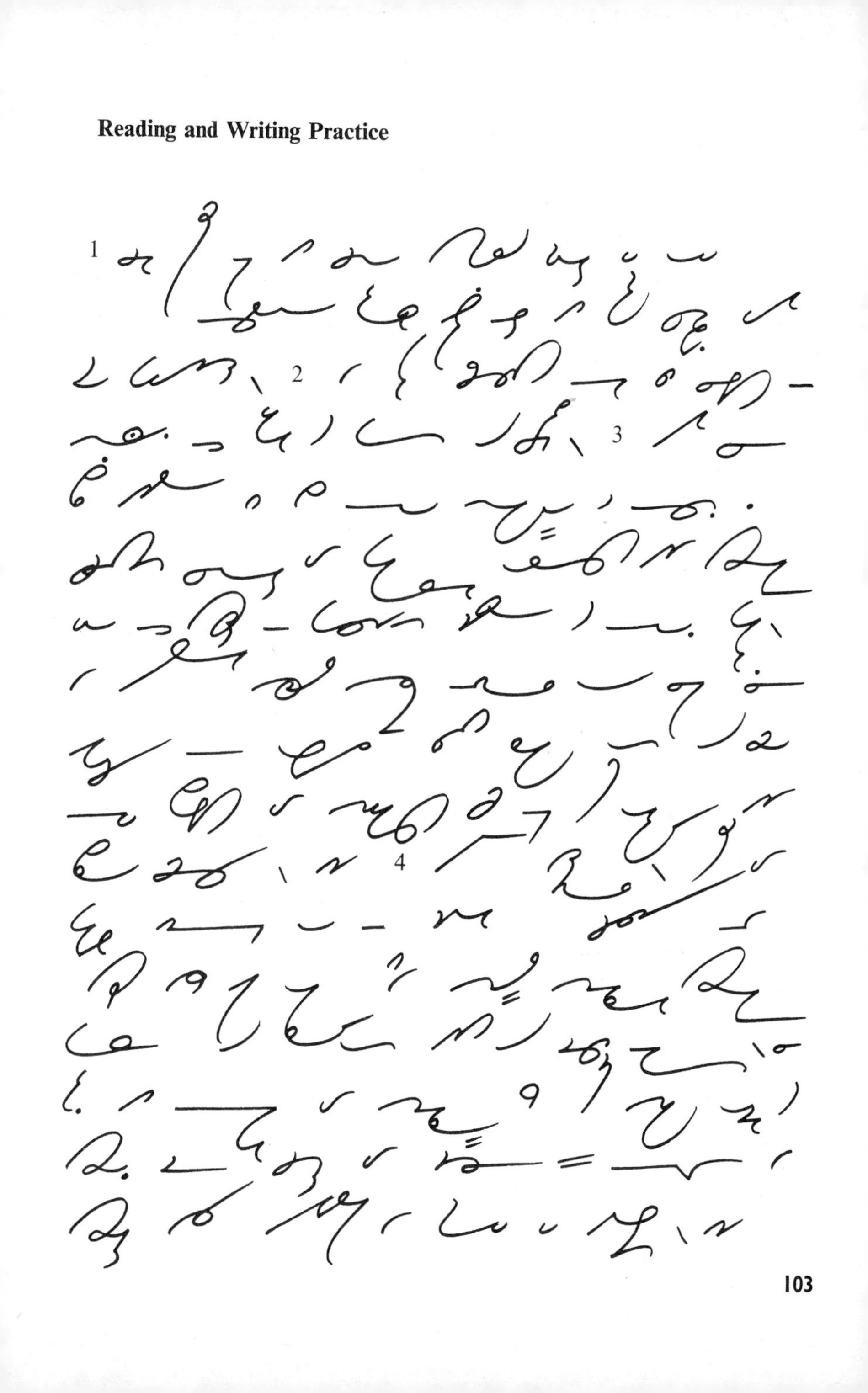

Reading and Writing Practice

Lesson 26

201. Word-beginning *electr-*

electric — electrician — electronics
electrical — electricity — electros
electrically — electronic — electrotype

202. Electric

electric cleaner — electric fan — electric light
electric iron — electric file — electric wire

203. Word-beginnings *inter-, intr-*

inter-

interfere — intermediate — interrupted
interference — internal — interruption
interim — international — interval
interior — interpreted — interview

intr-

introduce — introduction — intrusion

204. Word-beginnings *enter-, entr-*

enter — entering — entrance
entered — enterprise — entrant

205. Word-beginnings *short-, ship-*

short-

short — shortages — shorter
shortage — shorten — shortly

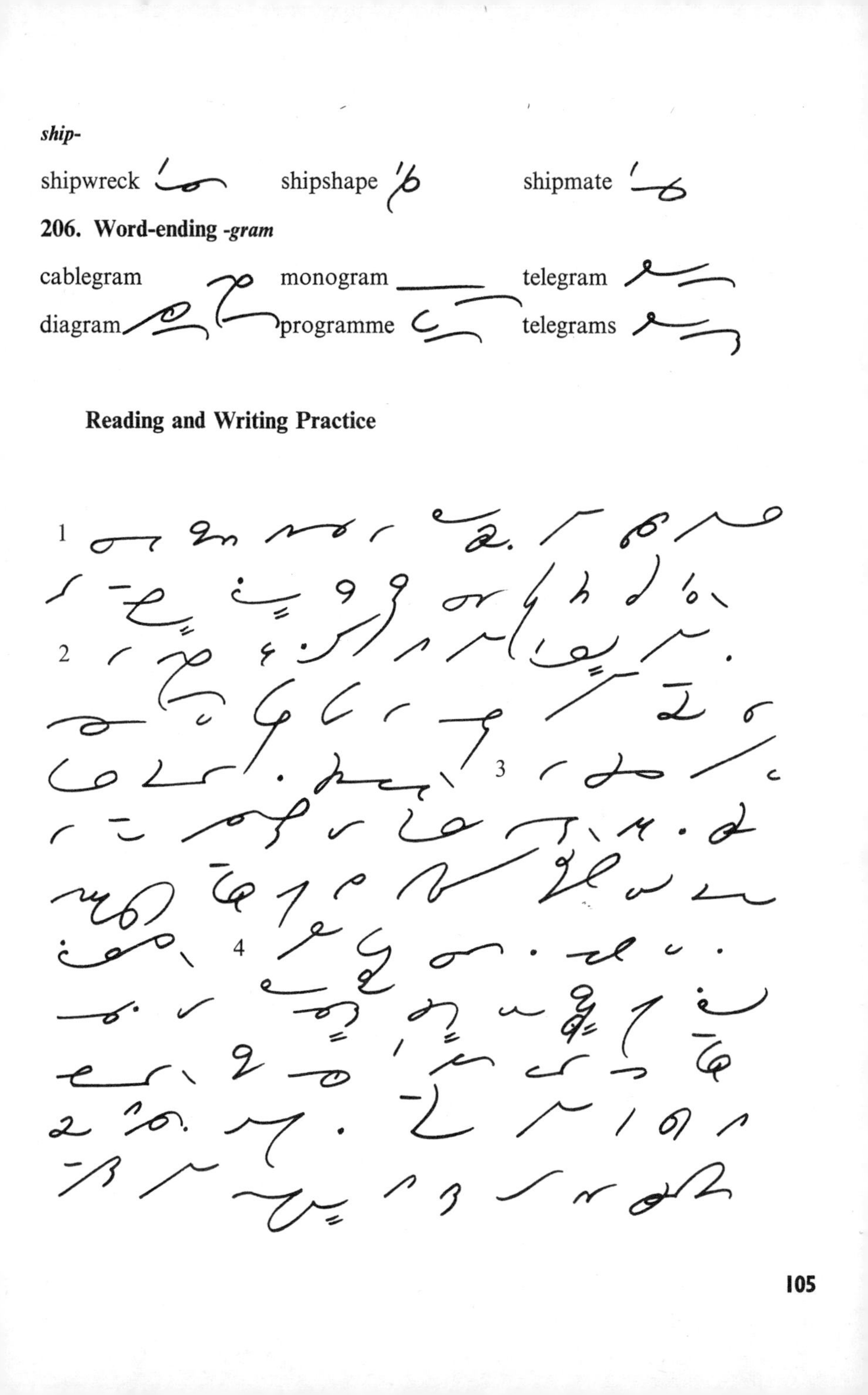

ship-

shipwreck shipshape shipmate

206. Word-ending *-gram*

cablegram monogram telegram

diagram programme telegrams

Reading and Writing Practice

1

2

3

4

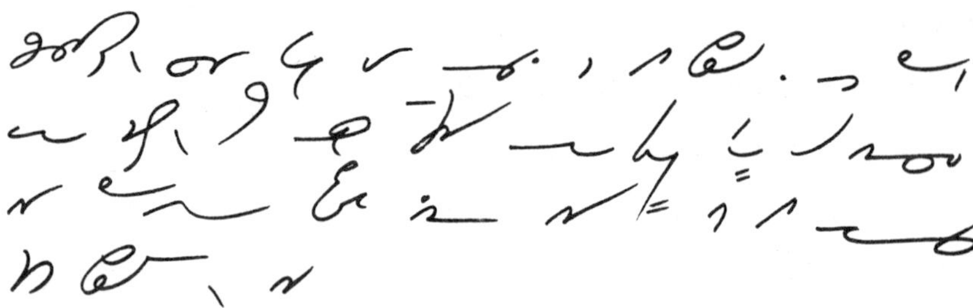

Lesson 27

211. Words modified in phrases

as soon as

as soon as possible

as soon as the

I hope

I hope that

I hope that the

I hope the

I hope these

I hope this

I hope to see

we hope

we hope that

we hope that these

we hope that this

we hope the

we hope these

we hope this

we hope to have

we hope you can

we hope you will

I had

I had been

I had not

let us

let us have

let us know

let us say

please let us

to us

to do

to do it

to do so

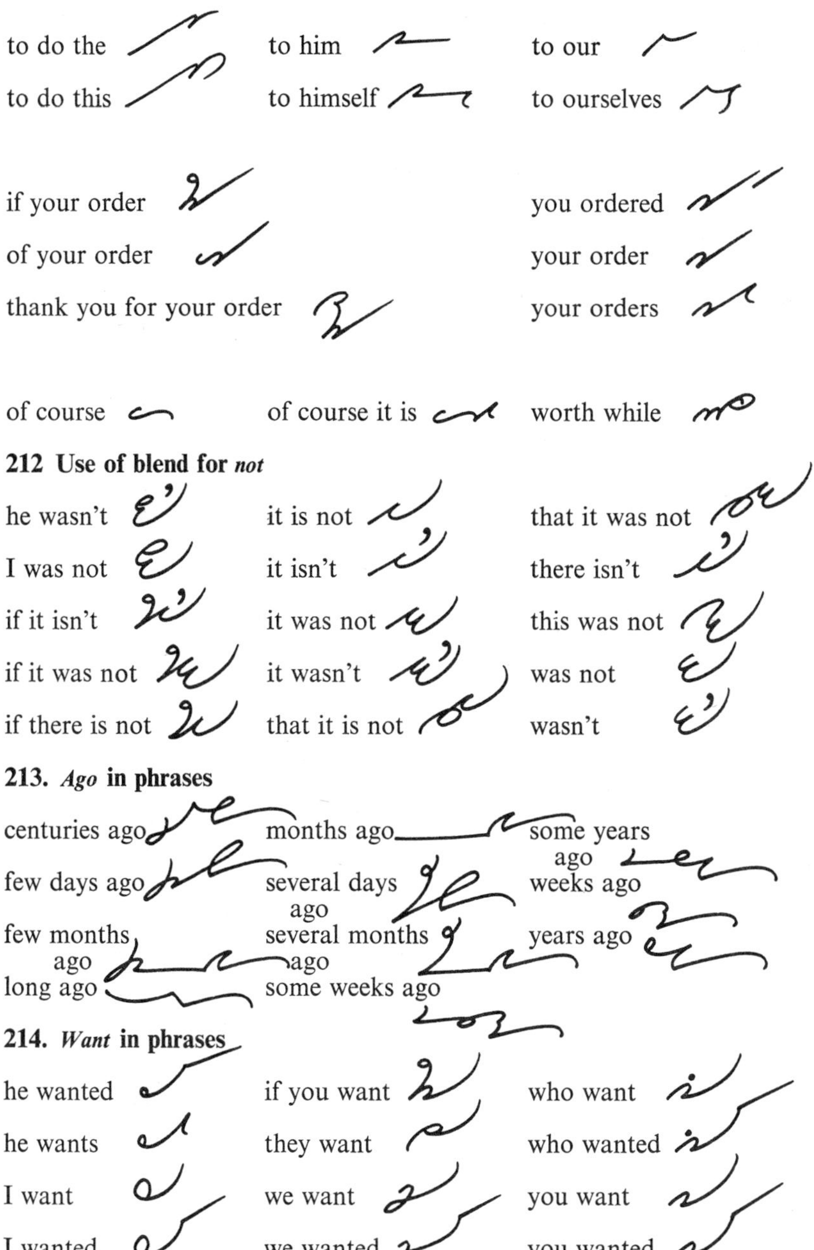

to do the
to do this
to him
to himself
to our
to ourselves

if your order
of your order
thank you for your order
you ordered
your order
your orders

of course
of course it is
worth while

212 Use of blend for *not*

he wasn't
I was not
if it isn't
if it was not
if there is not
it is not
it isn't
it was not
it wasn't
that it is not
that it was not
there isn't
this was not
was not
wasn't

213. *Ago* in phrases

centuries ago
few days ago
few months ago
long ago
months ago
several days ago
several months ago
some weeks ago
some years ago
weeks ago
years ago

214. *Want* in phrases

he wanted
he wants
I want
I wanted
if you want
they want
we want
we wanted
who want
who wanted
you want
you wanted

Reading and Writing Practice

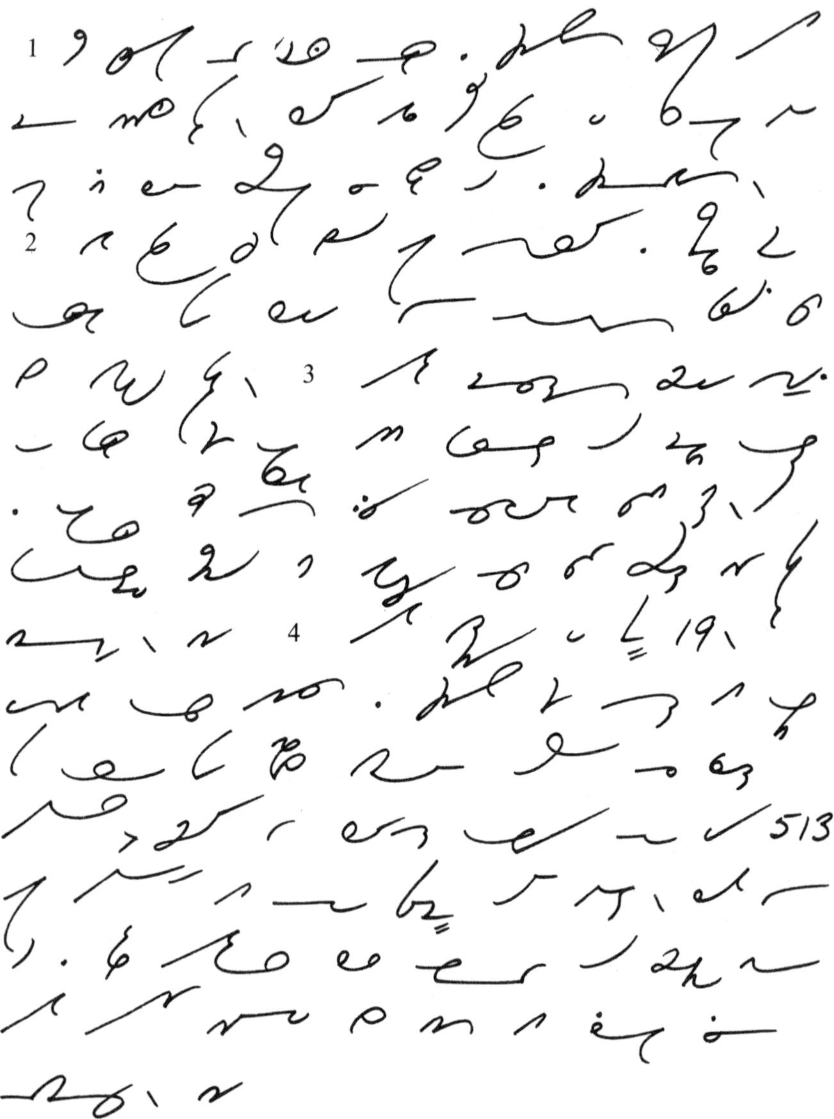

Lesson
28

219. Word-ending *-ful*

awful	doubtful	hopeful
beautiful	faithful	powerful
careful	grateful	thoughtful
carefully	helpful	useful
delightful	helpfulness	usefulness

220. Word-ending *-ify*

amplifier	diversified	notify
amplify	gratified	ratify
beautify	gratifying	specified
certified	justified	specify
certify	justify	testify
classified	modify	verify

220. Phrases

to beautify	to specify	to verify

221. Word-ending *-ification*

classification	modification	ratification
edification	notification	specifications
justification	qualifications	verification

222. Word-ending *-rity*

authorities	charity	clarity

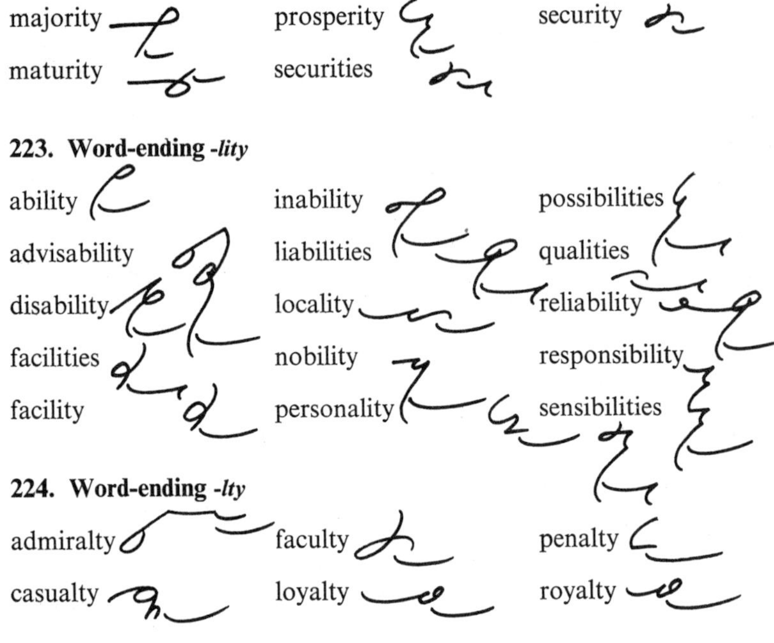

majority
maturity
prosperity
securities
security

223. Word-ending *-lity*

ability
advisability
disability
facilities
facility
inability
liabilities
locality
nobility
personality
possibilities
qualities
reliability
responsibility
sensibilities

224. Word-ending *-lty*

admiralty
casualty
faculty
loyalty
penalty
royalty

Reading and Writing Practice

4

A/2

Lesson 29

228. Blended consonants ***den***

abandon
accident
attendance
audience
danger
deny
dinner
evidence
evident
evidently
guidance
identical
identically
identification
identified
identify
precedence
president
residence
resident
student
sudden
tendency
wooden

229. Blended consonants *ten*

acceptance
attend
attended
attention
bulletin
button
carton
cotton
destined
distance
distant
extension
extensive

extensively
extent
hesitant
hesitancy
itinerary
lighten
maintenance
patent
retention
rotten
satin
sentence
standard

stenographer
stenographic
straighten
straightened
tenant
tend
tender
tendered
tent
tentative
tonight
utensil
written

230. Word-ending *-tain*

ascertain
attain
attainment
certain
certainly
certainty
curtain
detain

detained
entertain
entertainment
fountain
maintain
maintained
mountain
obtain

obtainable
obtained
pertaining
retain
retained
sustain
sustained
unobtainable

228-230. Phrases

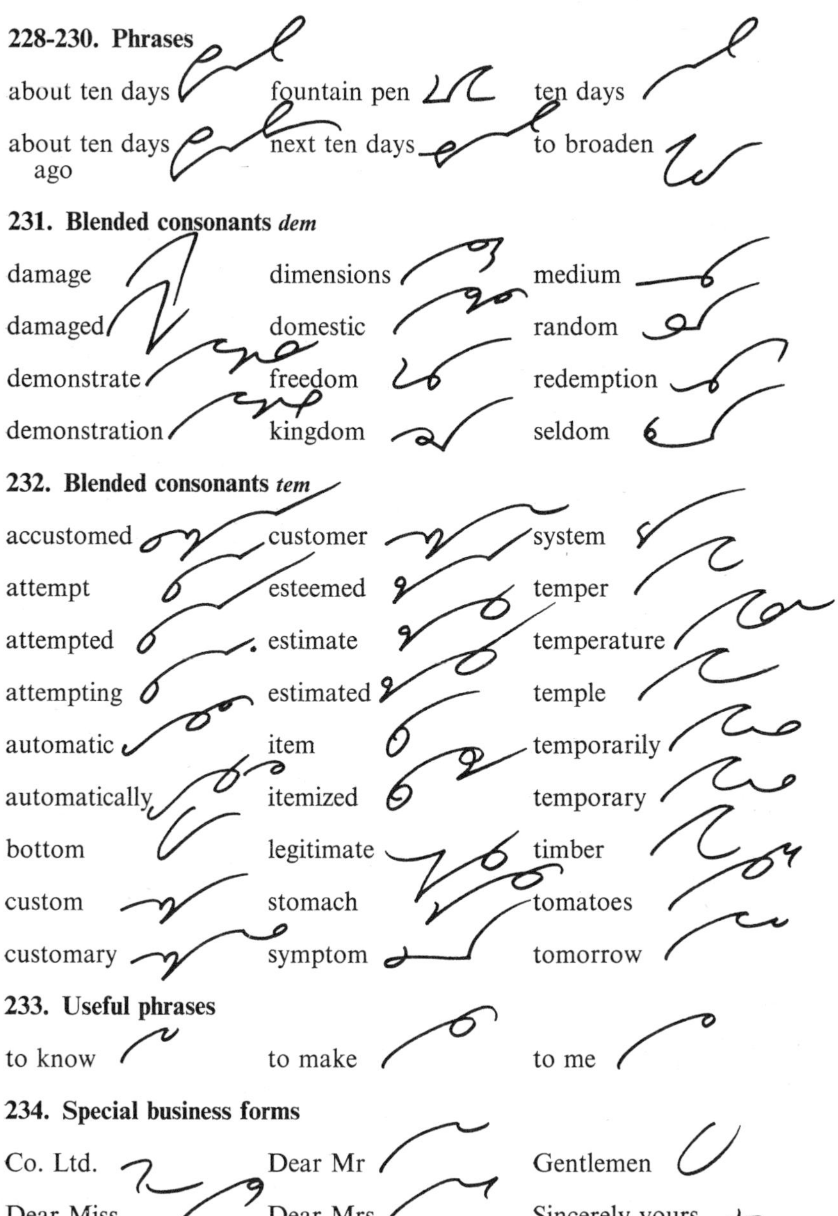

about ten days — fountain pen — ten days

about ten days ago — next ten days — to broaden

231. Blended consonants *dem*

damage — dimensions — medium

damaged — domestic — random

demonstrate — freedom — redemption

demonstration — kingdom — seldom

232. Blended consonants *tem*

accustomed — customer — system

attempt — esteemed — temper

attempted — estimate — temperature

attempting — estimated — temple

automatic — item — temporarily

automatically — itemized — temporary

bottom — legitimate — timber

custom — stomach — tomatoes

customary — symptom — tomorrow

233. Useful phrases

to know — to make — to me

234. Special business forms

Co. Ltd. — Dear Mr — Gentlemen

Dear Miss — Dear Mrs — Sincerely yours

Yours faithfully   Yours respectfully   Yours very sincerely

Very truly yours   Yours sincerely   Yours very truly

Reading and Writing Practice

1

2

3

4

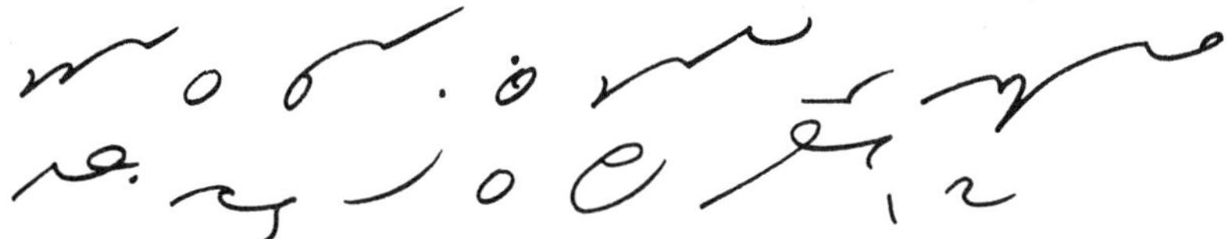

Lesson 30

238. Brief Forms

department	outstanding	sometimes
departure	part	stand
difficult	participate	standing
difficulty	parties	standpoint
extraordinary	party	stands
meantime	purchase	time
merchandise	purchased	times
merchant	purchases	understand
ordinarily	purchasing	understandable
ordinary	sometime	why

238. Phrases

about that time	at the time	each time
about the time	at this time	few times
about this time	at which time	for the time
after that time	before that time	from time
any time	by that time	in these times
at all times	by the time	in time
at that time	by this time	long time

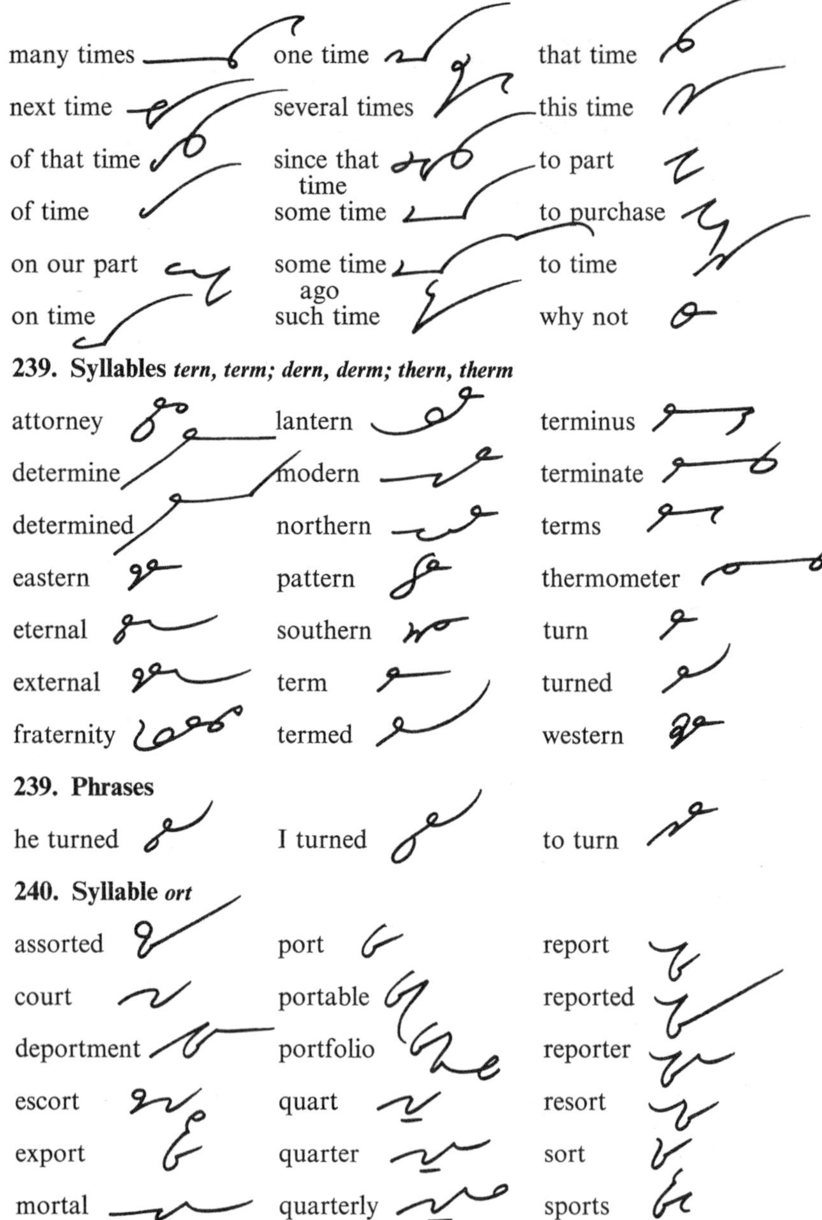

many times
one time
that time
next time
several times
this time
of that time
since that time
to part
of time
some time
to purchase
on our part
some time ago
to time
on time
such time
why not

239. Syllables *tern, term; dern, derm; thern, therm*

attorney
lantern
terminus
determine
modern
terminate
determined
northern
terms
eastern
pattern
thermometer
eternal
southern
turn
external
term
turned
fraternity
termed
western

239. Phrases

he turned
I turned
to turn

240. Syllable *ort*

assorted
port
report
court
portable
reported
deportment
portfolio
reporter
escort
quart
resort
export
quarter
sort
mortal
quarterly
sports

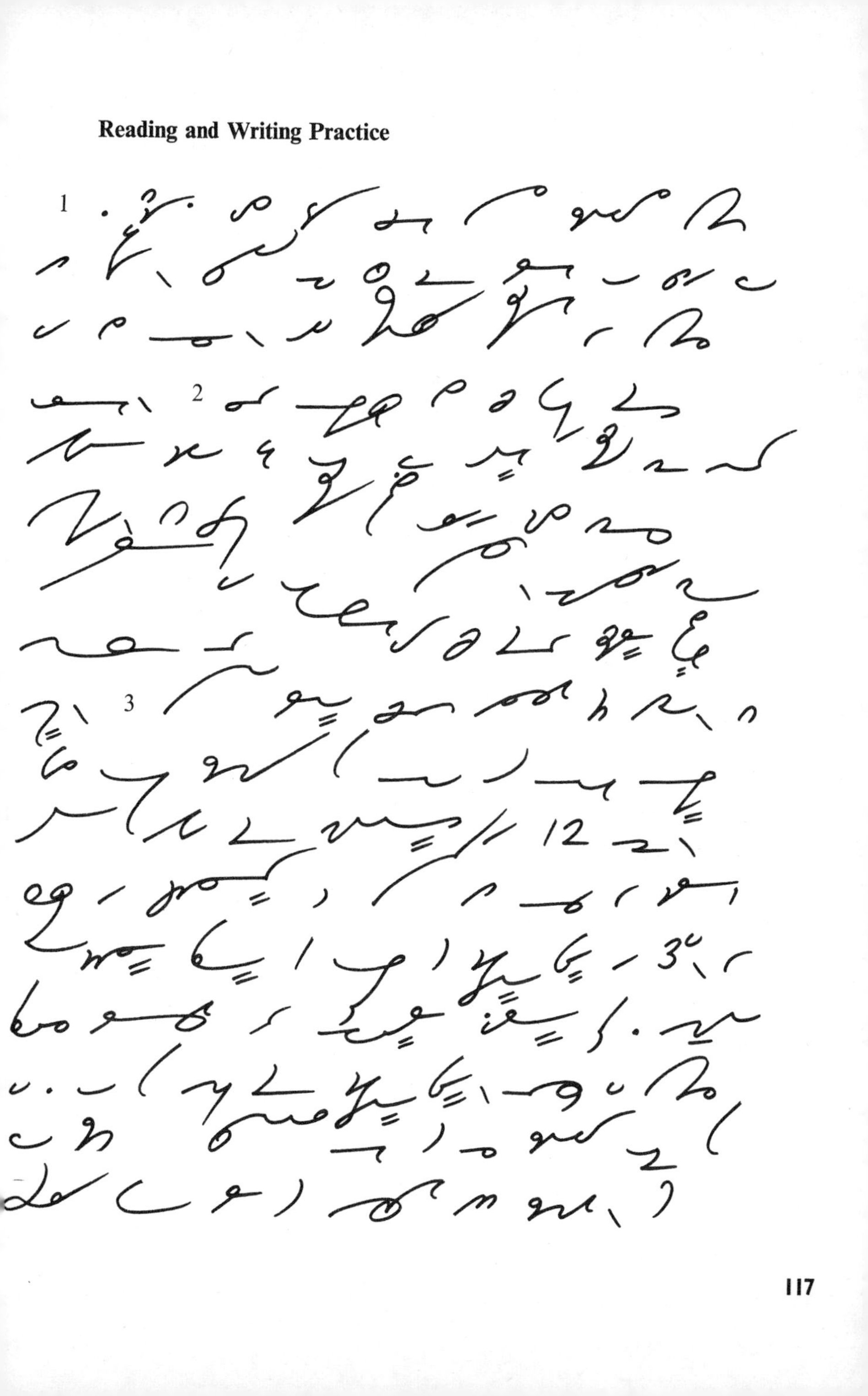

Reading and Writing Practice

1

2

3

Lesson 31 **CHAPTER SIX**

248. Omission of *t* in *-ct*

act	exact	product
collect	fact	protect
deduct	neglect	reflect
elect	predict	select

tract, trict, truct

abstract	extract	retract
attract	obstruct	strict
district	restrict	tract

fect, pect, ject

affect	expect	project
defect	perfect	prospect
effect	reject	respect

248. Phrases

affect the	fact that this	to perfect
fact that	in fact	to protect
fact that the	to collect	to select

249. Past tense, *-er, -or,* after *-ct*

actor	affected	collected

collector	neglected	rejected
deducted	protected	projector
expected	reflector	tractor

250. Other derivatives

active	exactly	productive
actively	expects	prospective
activity	expectations	prospectus
acts	facts	respectfully
affects	inactive	respective
attractive	perfectly	respectively
effectively	perfection	strictly

251. One-syllable words ending in *-st*

best	last	rested
cost	lasted	resting
costing	lasting	rests
costly	lasts	test
costs	past	tested
first	rest	tests

251. Phrases

at last	for the last	in the last
first class	for the past	last minute
first time	for the past year	last month

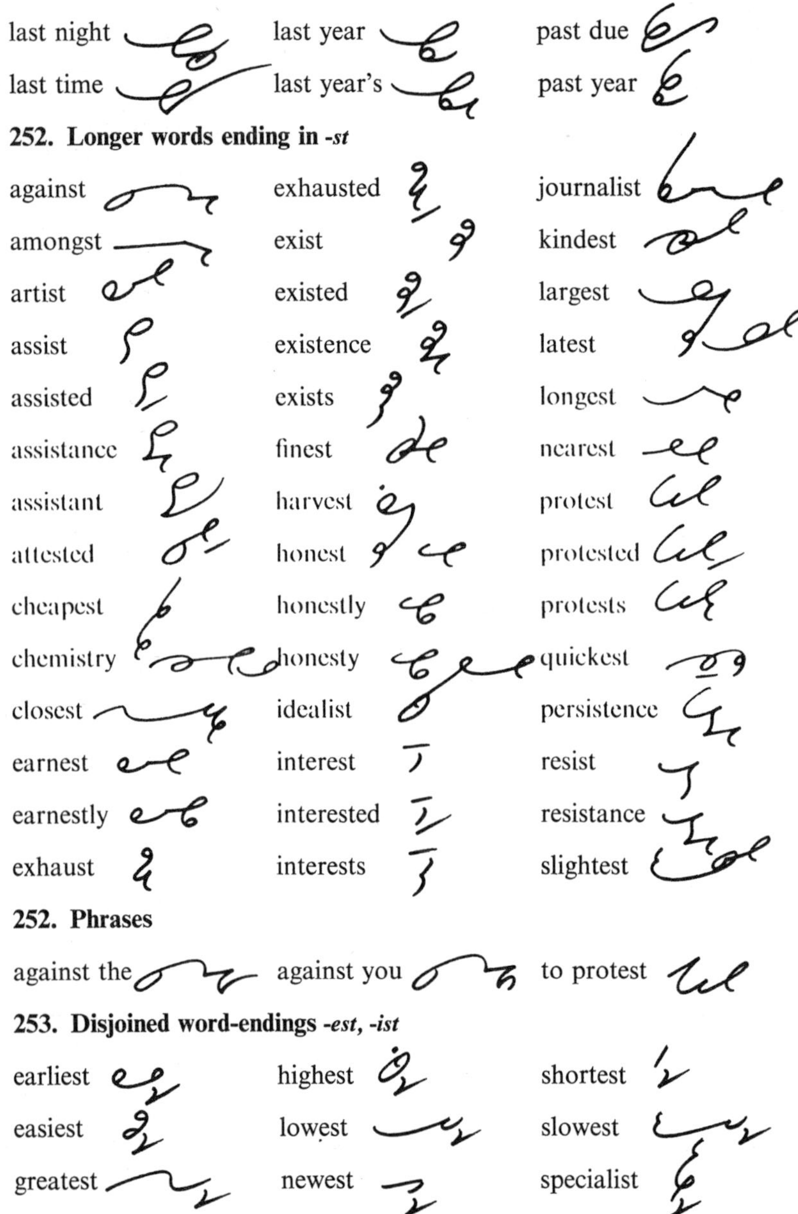

252. Longer words ending in *-st*

252. Phrases

253. Disjoined word-endings *-est, -ist*

Reading and Writing Practice

1 [shorthand]

2 [shorthand]

3 [shorthand]

4 [shorthand]

5 [shorthand]

Lesson
32

257. Brief Forms

advertise
advertised
advertiser
advertisement
body
consider
considerable
consideration
considerations
considered

else
elsewhere
estate
never
nobody
presence
present
presented
probable
probably

remember
represent
representative
represented
represents
somebody
state
stated
statement
states

257. Phrases

anyone else
anything else
at present
he considered
he considers
I consider
I remember

if you consider
into consideration
nobody else
nothing else
nowhere else
remember that
somebody else

someone else
something else
somewhere else
to consider
we shall consider
which we consider
you will remember

258. Omission of *d*

amend
amended
amendment

bound
bundles
demand
diamond
dividend
extend
extended
extends
mind
pound
pounds
recommend
recommended
remind
reminded

Reading and Writing Practice

1

2

3

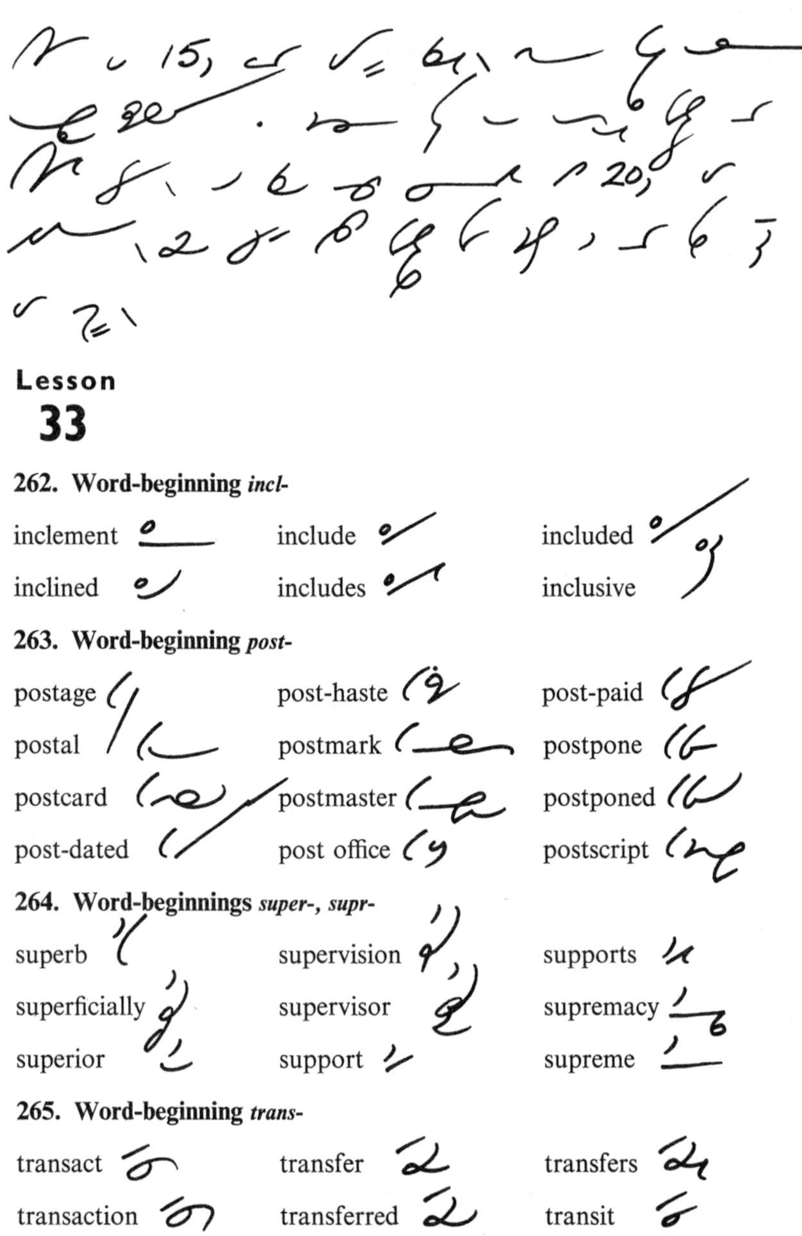

Lesson 33

262. Word-beginning *incl-*

inclement · include · included
inclined · includes · inclusive

263. Word-beginning *post-*

postage · post-haste · post-paid
postal · postmark · postpone
postcard · postmaster · postponed
post-dated · post office · postscript

264. Word-beginnings *super-, supr-*

superb · supervision · supports
superficially · supervisor · supremacy
superior · support · supreme

265. Word-beginning *trans-*

transact · transfer · transfers
transaction · transferred · transit

transition	transmit	transcribe
translated	transmitted	transcript
translation	transparent	transcription

Reading and Writing Practice

1

2

3

4

5

6

Lesson 34

269. Word-beginnings *con-, com-*

con-

concealed
concentrate
conception
concern
concerned
concert
concession
concrete
condense
condensed
conduct
conducted
conductor
confer
conference
confess
confidential
confine
confined
confirm
confirmed
conflict
congested
congestion
conjunction
connected
connexions
conscientious
consent
conservative
consign
consigned
consignee
consignment
consist
consisted
consistent
consistently
consists
consolidate
constant
constantly
construct
construction
constructive

contact	continue	convention
contain	continued	conversation
contained	continues	conversion
container	continuous	convert
contemplate	contract	converted
contemplated	contracted	convey
content	contractor	conveyance
contention	contracts	convince
contest	contrary	discontinue
continent	contrast	discontinued
contingent	control	reconcile
continuance	controversy	reconstruction

com-

accommodate	commitments	companion
accomplish	committed	comparative
accomplished	committee	compare
combine	commodities	compared
command	commodity	comparison
commence	common	compel
commend	commonly	compelled
comment	communities	compensation
commerce	community	compete
commercial	compact	competent

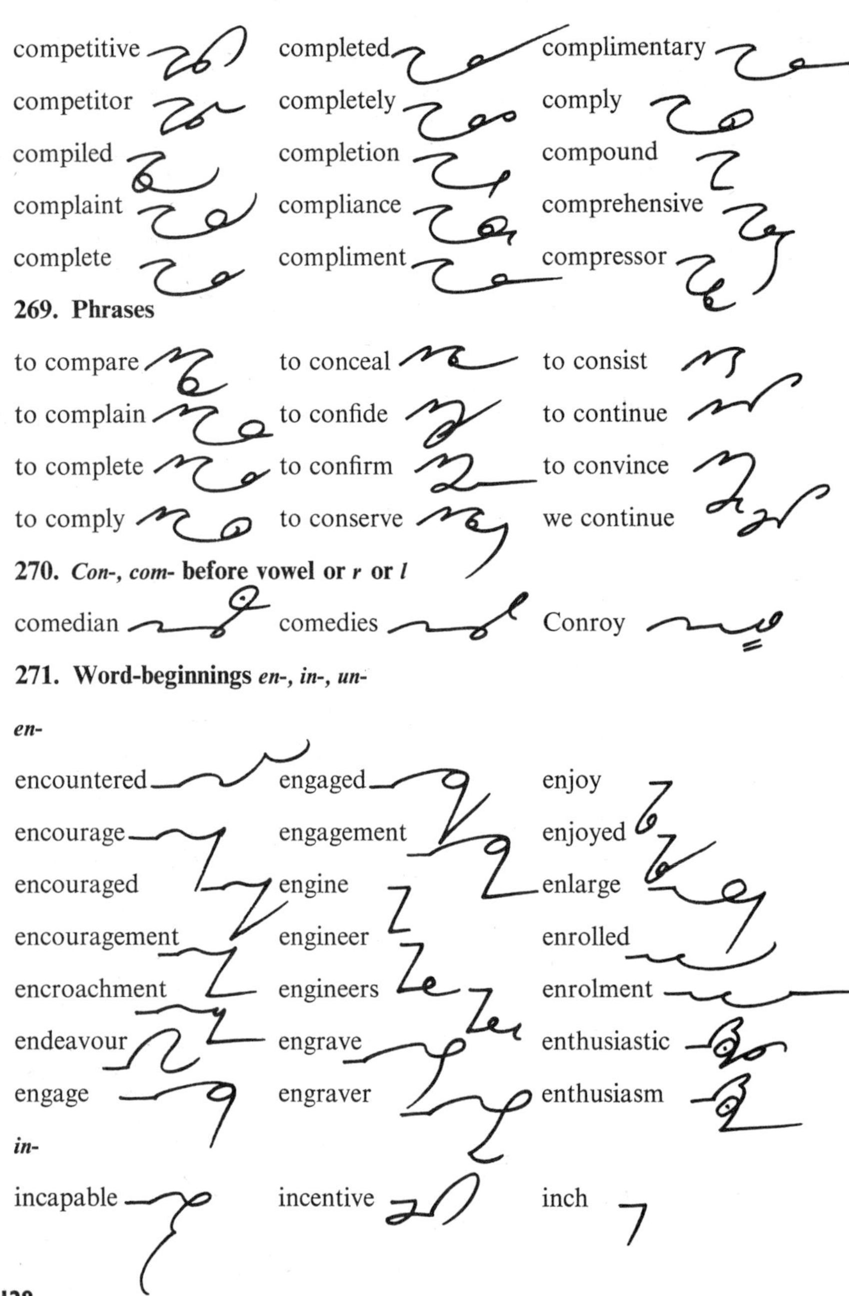

competitive
competitor
compiled
complaint
complete
completed
completely
completion
compliance
compliment
complimentary
comply
compound
comprehensive
compressor

269. Phrases

to compare
to complain
to complete
to comply
to conceal
to confide
to confirm
to conserve
to consist
to continue
to convince
we continue

270. ***Con-, com-*** **before vowel or** ***r*** **or** ***l***

comedian
comedies
Conroy

271. Word-beginnings ***en-, in-, un-***

en-

encountered
encourage
encouraged
encouragement
encroachment
endeavour
engage
engaged
engagement
engine
engineer
engineers
engrave
engraver
enjoy
enjoyed
enlarge
enrolled
enrolment
enthusiastic
enthusiasm

in-

incapable
incentive
inch

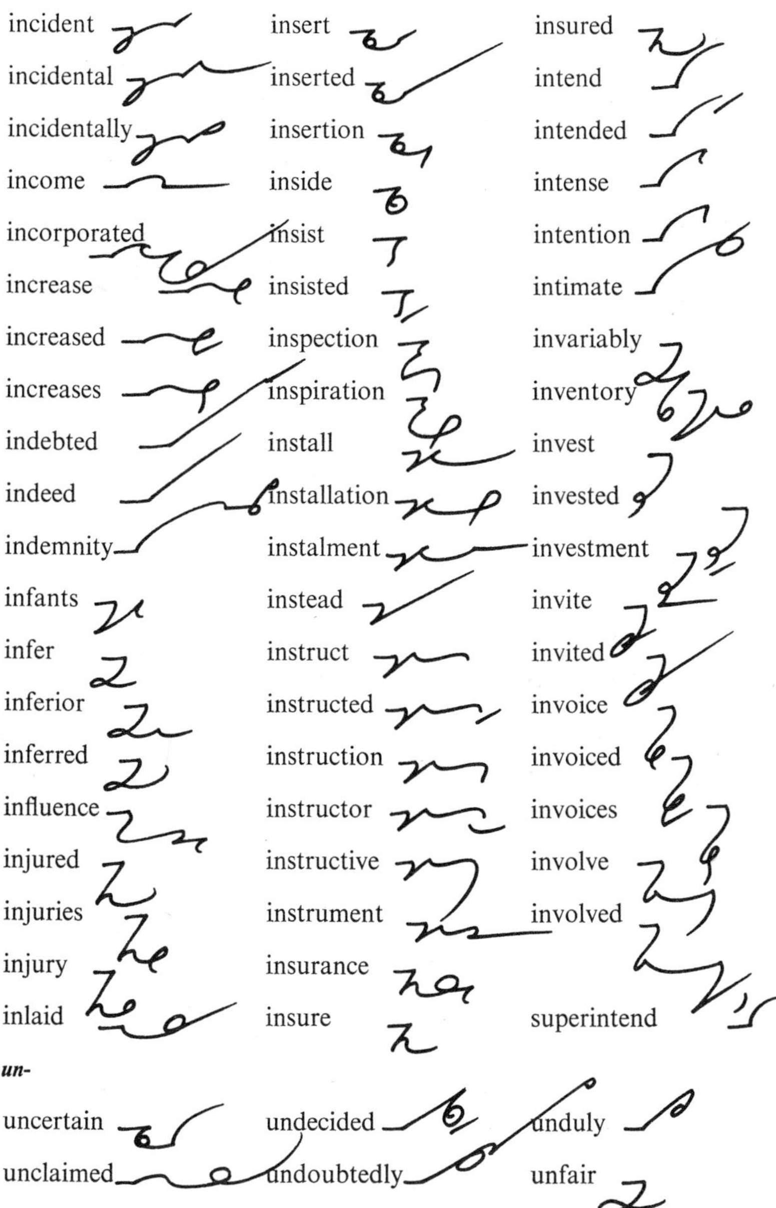

incident
incidental
incidentally
income
incorporated
increase
increased
increases
indebted
indeed
indemnity
infants
infer
inferior
inferred
influence
injured
injuries
injury
inlaid

insert
inserted
insertion
inside
insist
insisted
inspection
inspiration
install
installation
instalment
instead
instruct
instructed
instruction
instructor
instructive
instrument
insurance
insure

insured
intend
intended
intense
intention
intimate
invariably
inventory
invest
invested
investment
invite
invited
invoice
invoiced
invoices
involve
involved
superintend

un-

uncertain
unclaimed

undecided
undoubtedly

unduly
unfair

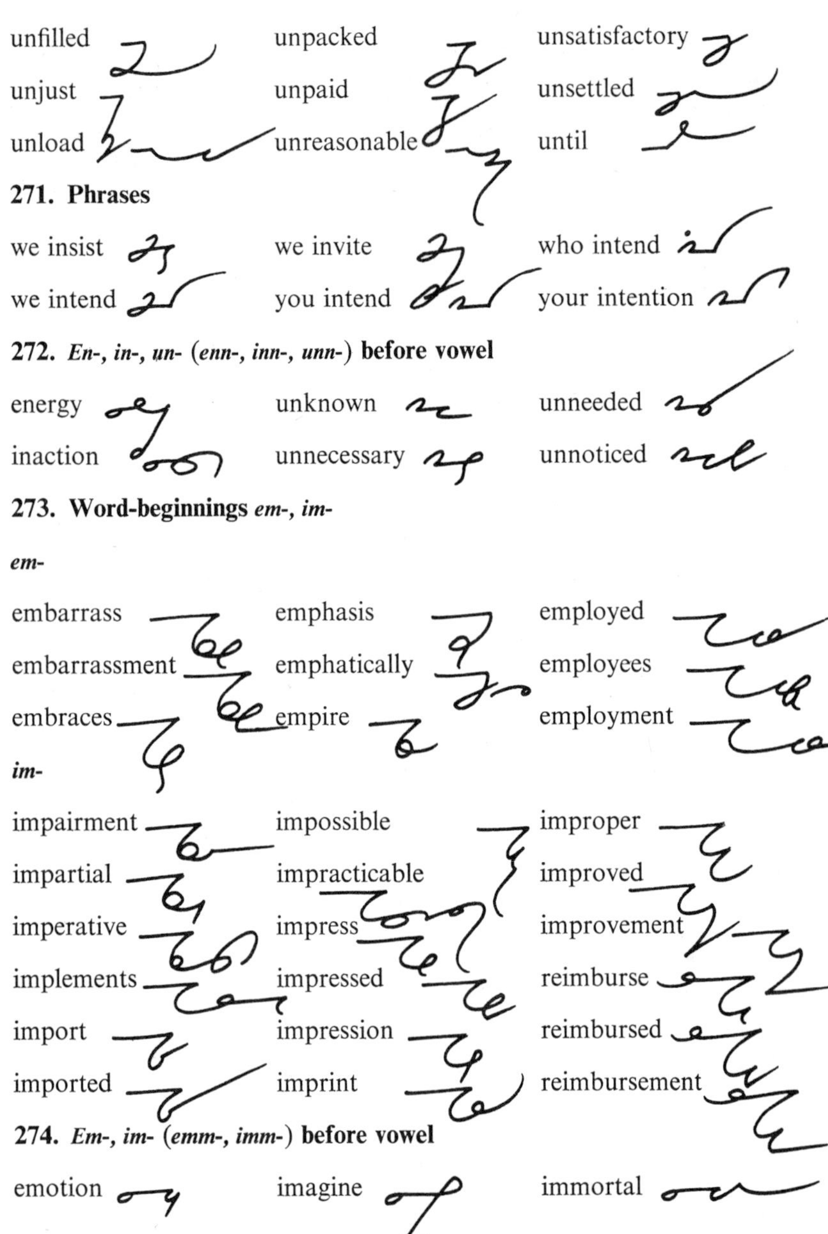

unfilled
unjust
unload
unpacked
unpaid
unreasonable
unsatisfactory
unsettled
until

271. Phrases

we insist
we intend
we invite
you intend
who intend
your intention

272. ***En-, in-, un-*** **(*enn-, inn-, unn-*) before vowel**

energy
inaction
unknown
unnecessary
unneeded
unnoticed

273. Word-beginnings *em-, im-*

em-

embarrass
embarrassment
embraces
emphasis
emphatically
empire
employed
employees
employment

im-

impairment
impartial
imperative
implements
import
imported
impossible
impracticable
impress
impressed
impression
imprint
improper
improved
improvement
reimburse
reimbursed
reimbursement

274. ***Em-, im-*** **(*emm-, imm-*) before vowel**

emotion
imagine
immortal

Reading and Writing Practice

Lesson 35

279. Word-ending *-hood*

boyhood hardihood neighbourhood
childhood manhood parenthood

280. Word-ending *-ward*

afterwards backward reward
awkwardly onward upward

281. Syllable *ul*

adult culminate resulted
agriculture culture resulting
consult multiple results
consulted result ultimate

282. Word-ending *-pose*

composed imposed presuppose
composer indisposed proposed
disposal opposed superimpose
disposed proposes supposed
exposed repose transpose

283. Word-ending *-position*

deposition position proposition
disposition positions propositions
exposition preposition supposition

281-283. Phrases

I suppose — to consult — to suppose

284-285. Word-endings ***-sume, -sumption***

assume — consumed — presumed

assumed — consumer — presumption

assumes — consumption — presumptive

assumption — presumably — resume

consume — presume — resumed

284-285. Phrases

I presume — presume that — presuming that

Reading and Writing Practice

5

6

Lesson 36

289. Brief Forms

acknowledge
acknowledged
acknowledgment
allow
allowance
allowed
future
idea

ideas
number
numbered
public
publication
publications
publicity
publish

published
publishers
quantities
quantity
regular
regularize
regularly
situation

289. Phrases

in this situation

to publish

290. Word-ending *-ulate*

accumulate

accumulated

accumulator

calculated

circulated

circulating

congratulate

cumulative

speculate

stimulate

stimulated

stimulates

290. Phrases

to calculate

to circulate

to speculate

291. Word-ending *-ulation*

accumulation

circulation

congratulations

population

speculation

tabulation

292. Word-ending *-ings*

bearings

beginnings

bookings

buildings

clippings

cuttings

dealings

drawings

earnings

evenings

feelings

filings

fittings

furnishings

greetings

hearings

holdings

linings

meetings

offerings

openings

paintings

railings

readings

proceedings

savings

sayings

stockings

things

winnings

292. Phrases

in this morning's — so many things — such things
many things — Friday morning's — this morning's

293. Word-ending *-ingly*

accordingly — feelingly — seemingly
approvingly — increasingly — unknowingly
exceedingly — knowingly — unwillingly

294. Word-ending *-less*

doubtless — hopeless — powerless
fearless — meaningless — priceless
heartless — motionless — unless
helplessly — needless — uselessly
helplessness — noiseless — worthless

295. Compound word-beginnings

disinclination — uncompromising — unenterprising
incomprehensible — uncontrollable — uninsured

Reading and Writing Practice

1

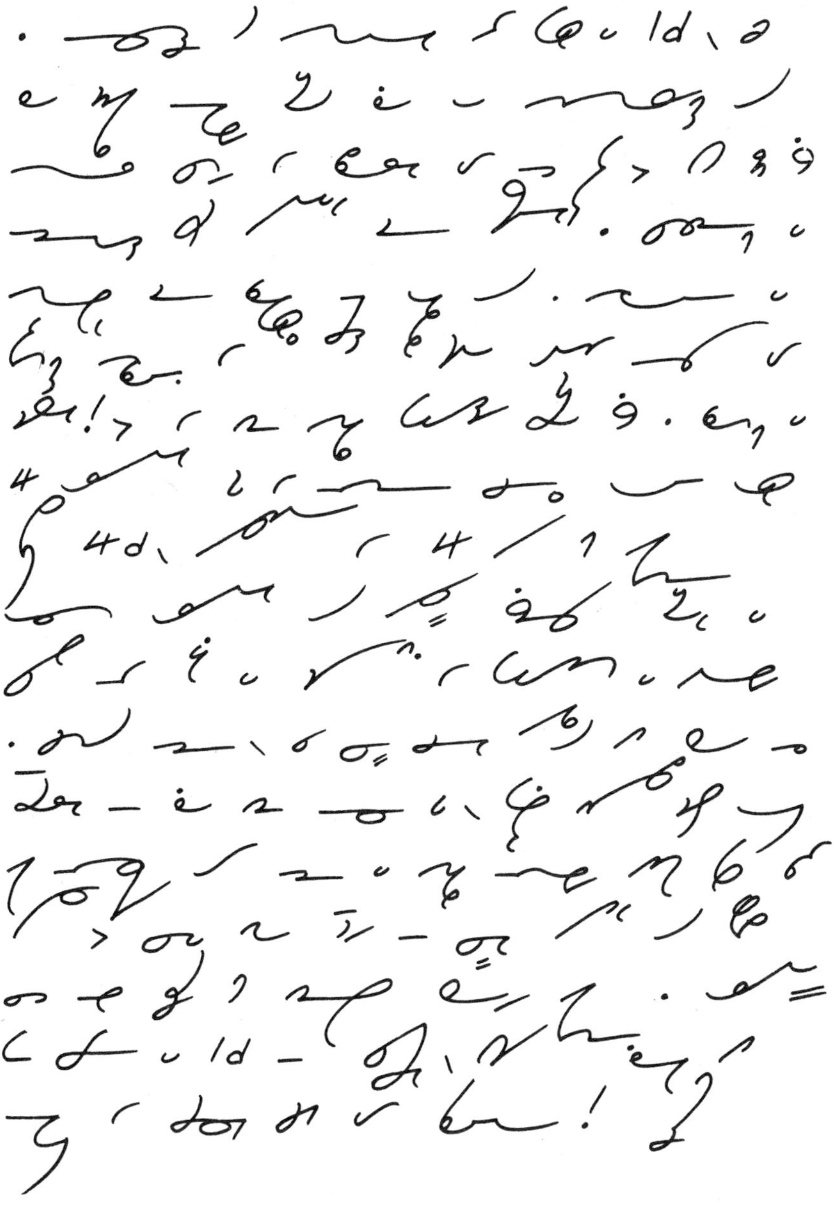

Lesson 37

CHAPTER SEVEN

304. Abbreviating principle

-use

accuse	confusing	inexcusable
accusation	confusion	refusal
confuse	excuse	refused
confused	excuses	refuses

-titude, -titute

aptitude	latitude	destitute
attitude	multitude	constitution
gratitude	constitute	institution

-cate

adequate	confiscate	indicates
advocate	duplicated	located
certificate	inadequate	reciprocated
communicate	indicated	syndicate

-cation

allocation	duplication	eradication
communication	education	indication
confiscation	educational	location

-gate

aggregate corrugated investigate

-gation

investigation irrigation obligation

304. Phrases

I refuse to confuse

Reading and Writing Practice

1

2

3

4

5

6

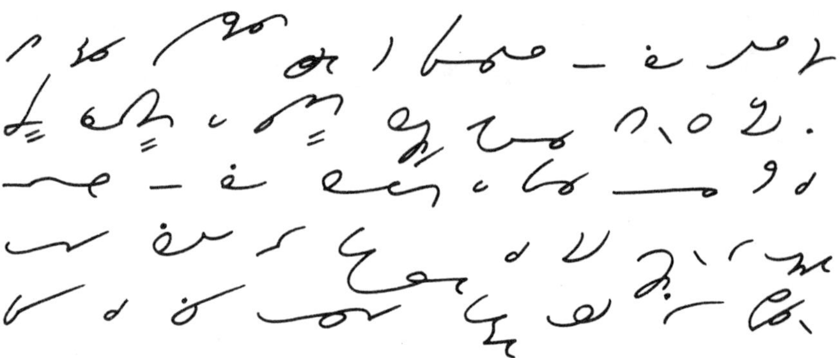

Lesson 38

309. Abbreviating principle (continued)

-quire

acquire | inquire | require
acquirement | inquiries | required
esquire | inquiry | requirements

-ntic

Atlantic | authentic | frantic

-ology

apologies | biology | psychological
apologize | physiology | technology
apology | psychology | terminology

-tribute

attribute | distributors | redistribution
contributed | distribution | retribution

-iety

propriety society variety

-quent, -quence

consequence delinquency frequently

consequently eloquence frequency

delinquent eloquent infrequent

-itis

appendicitis tonsillitis neuritis

Reading and Writing Practice

1

2

3

4

Lesson 39

313. Abbreviation—words not in families

algebra
alphabet
alphabetical
arithmetic
convenience
convenient
conveniently
curriculum
inconvenience
inconvenienced
inconvenient
equivalent
memoranda
memorandum
philosophy
preliminary
privilege
privileges
privileged
reluctant
significantly

314. Omission of circle before *-tion*

accommodation
addition
additional
admission
combination
commendation
commission
commissioner
competition
condition
confirmation
consolidation

consultation
destination
discrimination
donation
edition
estimation
examination
explanation
foundation

hesitation
imitation
interpretation
invitation
notation
omission
permission
petition
quotation

recommendation
repetition
reputation
solicitation
station
stationed
stationery
transmission
transportation

314. Phrases

in addition

to petition

Reading and Writing Practice

1

2

3

Lesson 40

318. Brief Forms

correct	discovery	newspaper
corrected	envelope	organization
correction	envelopes	organize
correctly	experience	regard
cover	experienced	regarded
covered	experiences	regardless
covers	inexperienced	regards
discovered	nevertheless	reorganize

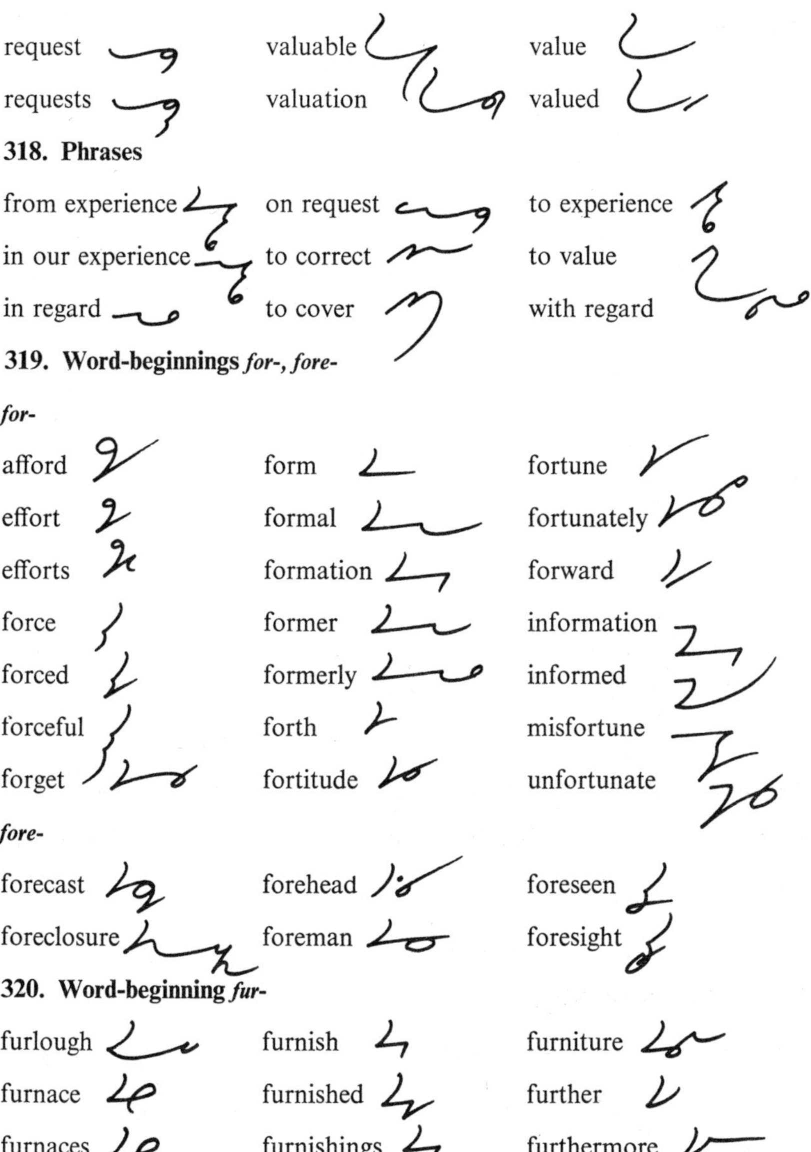

request	valuable	value
requests	valuation	valued

318. Phrases

from experience	on request	to experience
in our experience	to correct	to value
in regard	to cover	with regard

319. Word-beginnings *for-*, *fore-*

for-

afford	form	fortune
effort	formal	fortunately
efforts	formation	forward
force	former	information
forced	formerly	informed
forceful	forth	misfortune
forget	fortitude	unfortunate

fore-

forecast	forehead	foreseen
foreclosure	foreman	foresight

320. Word-beginning *fur-*

furlough	furnish	furniture
furnace	furnished	further
furnaces	furnishings	furthermore

319-320. Phrases

any information	to force	to form
informing us	to foresee	to forward
inform you	to forget	to furnish
setting forth	to forgo	to perform

321. Word-beginning *al-*

almanac	alter	alternations
almost	altered	alternatives
already	alteration	although
also	alternately	altogether

322. Word-beginning *sub-*

subchief	submit	subsequently
subdivide	submitted	substance
subdivision	subordinate	substantial
subeditor	subscribe	substantially
subhead	subscriber	substantiate
sublet	subscription	subtracted
submission	subsequent	subway

323. Word-beginning *self-*

self-contained	self-educated	self-sacrifice
self-control	self-made	self-satisfied
self-defence	self-pity	self-styled
selfishness	self-respect	self-supporting

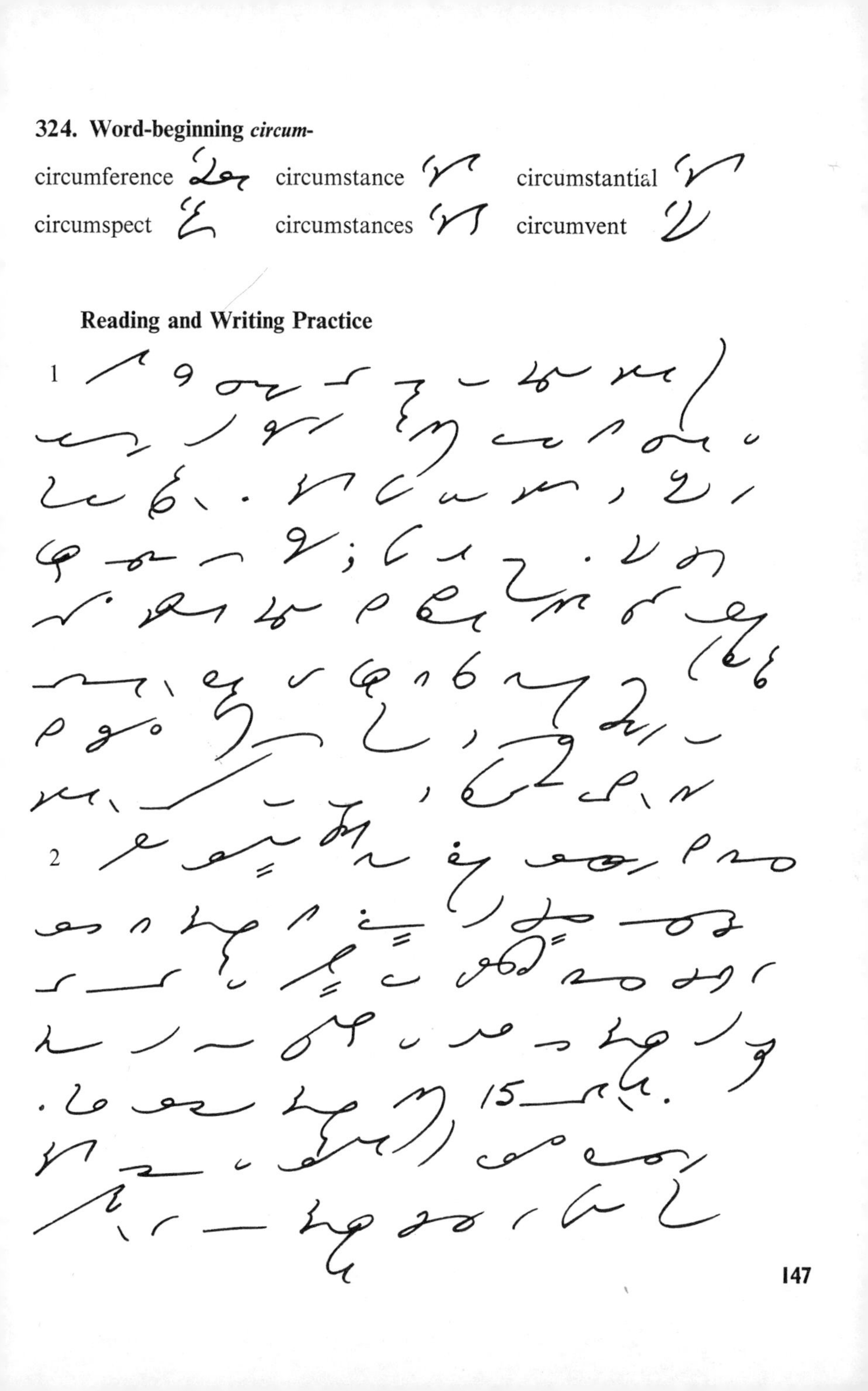

324. Word-beginning *circum-*

circumference circumstance circumstantial

circumspect circumstances circumvent

Reading and Writing Practice

1

2

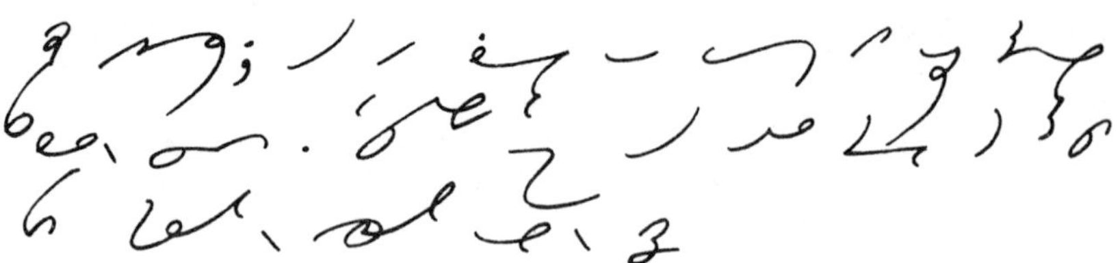

Lesson 41

328. Words omitted in phrases

able to say	I should like to have
as a result	I should like to know
at a loss	in a few days
at a time	in a few months
at such a time	in addition to the
bill of sale	in addition to this
by the way	in order to be
during the last	in order to become
during the past	in relation to the
for a few days	in such a manner
for a few minutes	in the future
for a long time	in the market
for a minute	in the past
for a moment	in the world
glad to have	line of business
glad to know	line of work
glad to say	many of the

many of them	out of them
men and women	out of this
more and more	out of town
more or less	should like to have
none of the	should like to see
none of them	some of our
on the market	some of the
one of our	some of them
one of the	some of these
one of the best	some of those
one of the most	son-in-law
one of them	such a thing
one of these	two or three
one of those	up and down
one or two	up to date
out of date	we should like to have
out of that	week or two
out of the	will you please
out of the way	will you please see

329. Phrases with *understand, understood*

actually understand	definite understanding
better understanding	definitely understood
clearly understood	do you understand

easily understand

friendly understanding

has understood

I could understand

I do not understand

I understand

it is understood

misunderstanding

misunderstood

mutual understanding

my understanding

our understanding

please understand

readily understand

readily understood

to understand

we cannot understand

we hope you will understand

we understand

we understand that

we understood

with the understanding

you do not understand

you will understand

Reading and Writing Practice

1

2

3

4

5 27

6

Lesson 42

333. Brief Forms

agent	director	questions
agents	directors	throughout
between	enough	unquestionably
direct	immediate	unquestioned
directed	immediately	wonder
direction	opinion	wondered
directly	question	wonderful

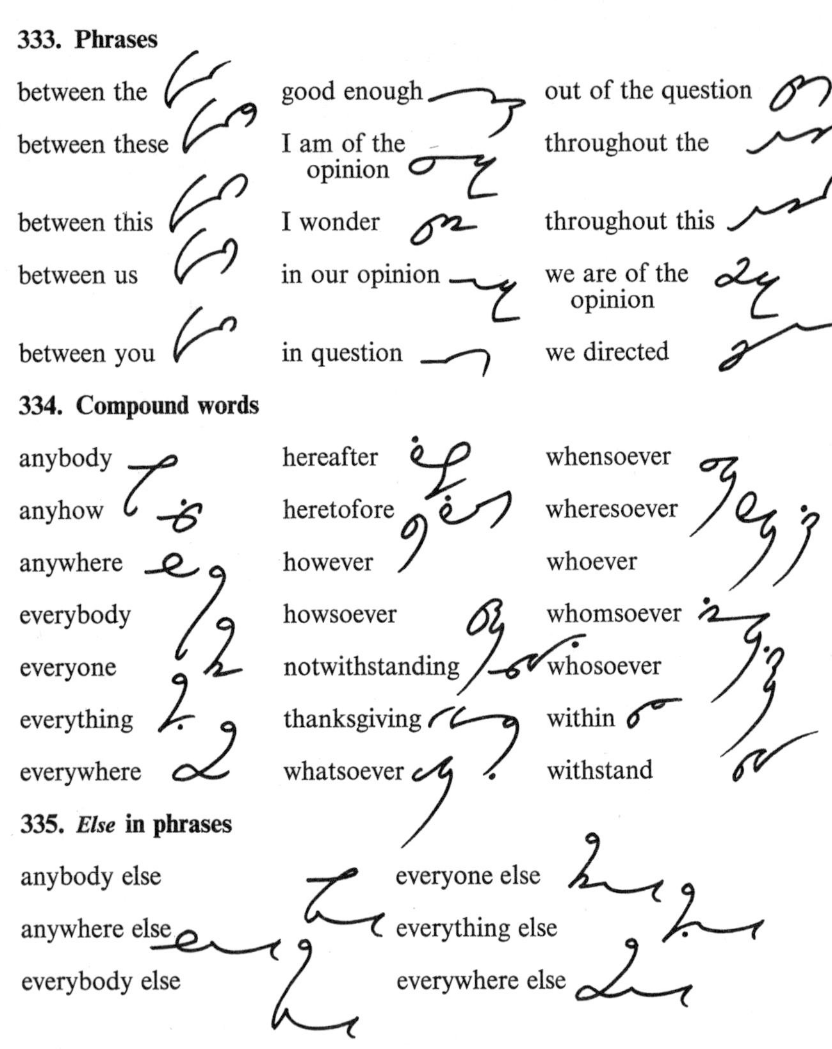

333. Phrases

between the
between these
between this
between us
between you
good enough
I am of the opinion
I wonder
in our opinion
in question
out of the question
throughout the
throughout this
we are of the opinion
we directed

334. Compound words

anybody
anyhow
anywhere
everybody
everyone
everything
everywhere
hereafter
heretofore
however
howsoever
notwithstanding
thanksgiving
whatsoever
whensoever
wheresoever
whoever
whomsoever
whosoever
within
withstand

335. *Else* in phrases

anybody else
anywhere else
everybody else
everyone else
everything else
everywhere else

Reading and Writing Practice

1

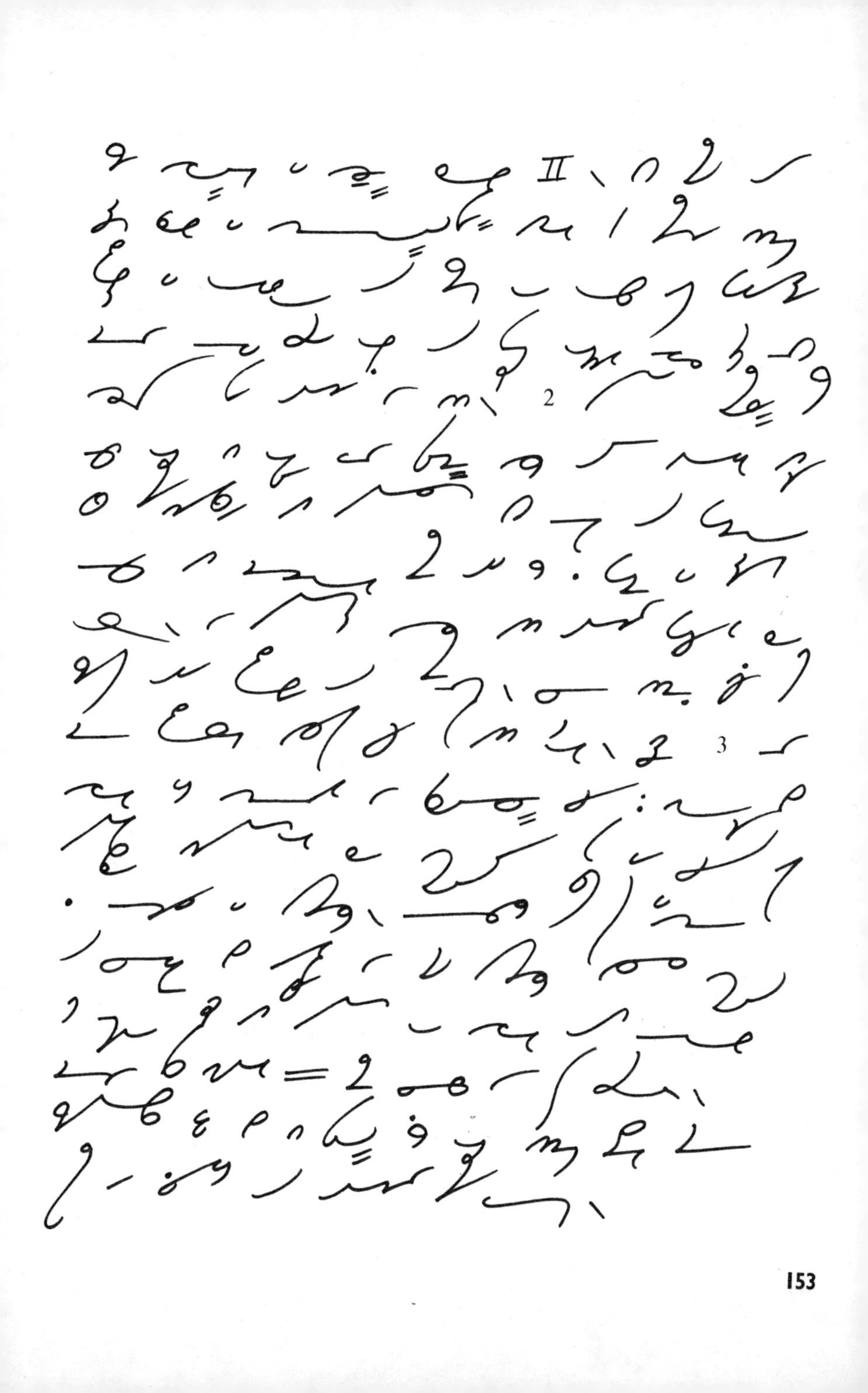

2

3

Lesson
43

CHAPTER EIGHT

342. Brief Forms

conclude	houses	references
concluded	object	referred
conclusion	objected	referring
conclusive	objection	refers
confidence	particular	subject
confident	particularly	success
house	particulars	successes
housed	refer	successful
household	reference	warehouse

342. Phrases

in conclusion	on the subject
in particular	to which you refer
in reference	with reference
in reference to your letter	with reference to the

343. Quantities—phrases

per gallon   per hundredweight   per pound

344. Intersection

Chamber of Commerce   c.o.d.   vice versa

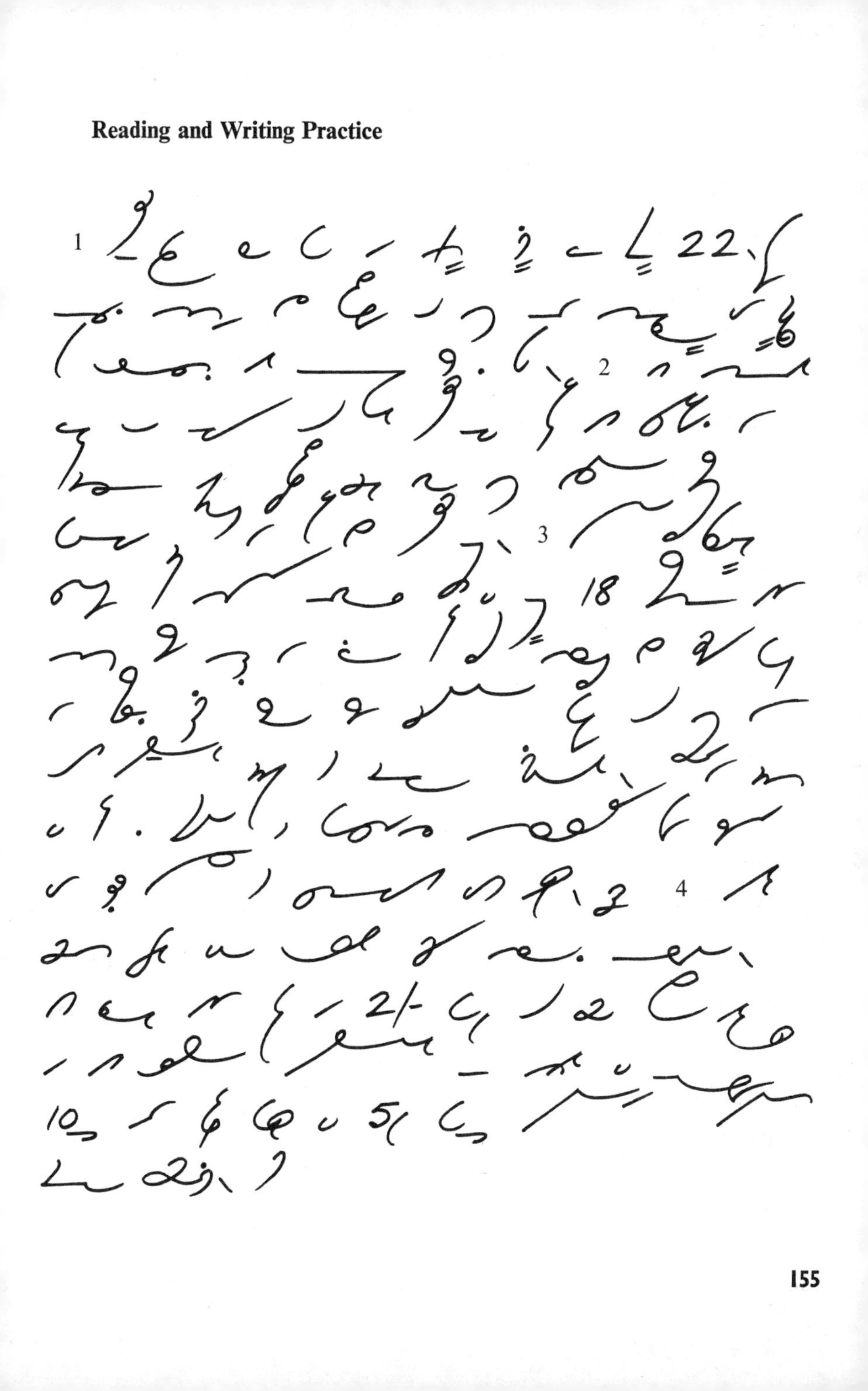

Reading and Writing Practice

1

2

3

4

Lesson 44

349. Brief Forms

advantage
advantages
advantageous
correspond
correspondence
corresponding
disadvantage
etc.
instance
instant
likewise
otherwise
railway
railways
recognition
recognize
recognized
yesterday

349. Phrases

for instance
in this instance

350. Proper-name terminations

-port

Bridport
Devonport
Gosport
Maryport
Southport
Stockport

-field

Butterfield
Chesterfield
Greenfield
Hatfield
Macclesfield
Mansfield
Stansfield
Sheffield
Wakefield

-chester

Barchester
Chichester
Colchester
Dorchester
Rochester
Winchester

-borough

Edinburgh	Jedburgh	Middlesbrough
Fraserburgh	Knaresborough	Peterborough
Gainsborough	Marlborough	Scarborough

-ford

Ashford	Brentford	Oxford
Bradford	Ilford	Stamford

-ington

Accrington	Leamington	Washington
Burlington	Warrington	Wellington

-ingham

Birmingham	Cunningham	Nottingham
Buckingham	Gillingham	Rockingham

Reading and Writing Practice

1

2

Lesson
45

355. Brief Forms

automobile	circular	government
character	encircle	prosecute
characteristic	encircled	prosecuted
characters	govern	prosecution
circle	governed	remainder

355. Phrases

to govern

to prosecute

356. Geographical abbreviations

America	Glasgow	New Zealand
American	Great Britain	New York
British Isles	Ireland	Scotland
Canada	Liverpool	U.K.
Canadian	London	U.S.
England	Manchester	U.S.A.
English	Newfoundland	U.S.S.R.

Reading and Writing Practice

1

2

3

CHAPTER ONE

LESSON 3

1. I am making a claim.
2. Her good advice helped me in preparing the claim.
3. The retail dealer has given me a cheque.
4. Place the medals in the safe at night.
5. Our team made a good showing in the game at East Road.
6. He came here in an hour, arriving an hour ago.
7. A little saving each day will make a large total.
8. Our girls are favouring neater hair styles.
9. I am mailing her a birthday greeting.
10. Our trading in these goods will show a clear gain.
11. I agree, so I would vote in favour.
12. Will the man go at Easter?
13. No, he may get a rise in May, so he will not leave the firm's service.
14. Saving as a habit will give him more capital.
15. He might stay at the farm an hour or more, arriving here a good deal later in the evening.
16. She typed a brief note in haste, hoping it would catch the night mail.

LESSON 4

1. I can see no case for adopting the less popular line.
2. Shall I give the marked price for the clock if I cannot get it at a cheaper rate?
3. I know I could get a better model by having a thinner copper lining.
4. Rob Smith will be selling off his stock of clothing at his shop in Dock Road.
5. My daughter will need help with the filing job.
6. By crossing the road in haste, she caused the driver of the car a good deal of alarm before he could stop.
7. I lost my keys so could not operate the lock.
8. The readers he asked for are not in stock, but there are large supplies of the blotting pads on sale.
9. Miss Church has taken a lot of care in preparing these broadcasts.
10. These odd samples can be put in the catalogue marked at a moderate price.
11. As I am taking my daughter abroad for her health, leaving on May 12, I shall not be at the meeting in aid of our hospital.

LESSON 5

1. I broke these glasses an hour ago.
2. It will necessitate buying more lenses.
3. Can he get a list of the taxes from these sources?

4. The addresses are to be put in the spaces here.
5. Our store is offering silk goods at bargain prices.
6. He put the boxes of mixed creams in his pocket.
7. The tax which I shall have to pay by May 31 is being assessed.
8. Notices of the changed services will appear in the evening papers.
9. Her niece is going in a taxi to visit the nurses at the hospital.
10. I need to have an analysis of our trading losses.
11. There is no basis for criticism of these losses before the real causes are assessed.
12. His daughter says he will sign the leases for the premises at Main Road.
13. There are good chances of our being given places in the team to play the Navy.
14. The Navy versus Army Services will be a fine game to see.
15. There are three clauses to which I cannot agree in the draft lease. These will have to be changed.

LESSON 6

1. Mark hopes to sell these cabinets before he goes north as he is in need of ready cash.
2. Miss Small made no charge for her services at the Sale which she arranged in aid of the Road Safety Campaign.
3. I am sorry my daughter cannot be at the meeting. She hurt her leg in falling off a horse.
4. There is a bad fault in the material. I would say the machine needs to have a thorough check.
5. The hospital broadcast made an appeal for nurses. Training would be given free with a little cash for the pocket.
6. I shall get a thicker material for the bag. There is a good-class line at the large store in College Road, but it is by no means cheap.
7. I hear with regret James Stone is leaving our firm. The staff are making him a gift of an easy chair.
8. Paul is the author of an original story which I read in our journal. Its principal setting is a belt of territory in the Near East. There is a copper mine which is the scene of a daring robbery. Has the guilty man left no trace by which he can be tracked? The cashier making a thorough search is able to supply the vital thread of knowledge by means of which the fellow is caught at the finish. I could not stop reading this absorbing story.

CHAPTER TWO

LESSON 7

1. My season ticket expires in a day or so.
2. For the extra journey I shall have to pay excess fare.
3. A thorough knowledge will expedite the gaining of expert skill.
4. Mr Smith's speech expressed the feeling of the meeting.
5. Our chief clerk will write them

a note to explain that these expenses were charged in error.
6. In making so extreme a claim her desires exceed her legal rights.
7. Their charge for extras for the year was thought to be excessive.
8. Our firm will spare no expense on the exterior finish of the premises.
9. Each exhibit must be ready by March 31 except those in the packaging class, which have an extra day.
10. It can be expensive to you if you drive your car too fast so that you exceed the speed limit, since you may have to pay a fine.
11. Dear Madam, If you desire to have a less expensive car, our Mr Box could help you in arranging an exchange. Yours truly,
12. Dear Sirs, Your policy will expire on May 15. May I have your cheque by express post? Yours truly,

LESSON 8

1. I must have the right to a cancellation of the deal at my option before May 12.
2. The posting official asked if the initials on the package were yours.
3. She agrees with me that an inexpensive coat might serve for social occasions if the selection is made with care.
4. It is the fashion in these days to try to dodge taxation, but taxes are essential to finance the protection of the nation as well as for the social services.
5. As Mr Dix has had a thorough preparation for teaching, he has been given exemption from Section 5.
6. Extreme caution in driving his car is the method that Mr Smith adopts for the prevention of collisions.
7. An authorization for these financial operations will be given if you make a special application before March 15.
8. Dear Madam, Our session closes on May 31. It will be followed by a brief vacation. Yours truly,
9. Dear Sir, Before you could get possession of the premises, you would have to agree to clause 7. Action must be taken before the expiration of the lease. Yours truly,

LESSON 9

1. These classes were specially arranged to meet the needs of totally or partially deaf people.
2. Lately Mr Bradley has been able to read only the financial page of his daily paper.
3. The change was highly pleasing to them, especially to the wholesale section of the trade.
4. I am sincerely pleased to learn from your note that the family are in good health.
5. When your answers are given clearly, simply, briefly, you will then be able to gain higher marks.
6. I have been advised by them that they will closely follow the agreed plan.
7. When elections take place

nationally or locally, you should not omit to vote.

8. It is better to be early than late, but occasionally "more haste" may mean "less speed."

9. Mr Hale: Please check thoroughly from these census figures the data in relation to families. As originally arranged, the figures were to have been shown separately, but I should like to change the plan slightly in the hope of getting the job finished earlier.

LESSON 10

1. I was late in trying to reserve seats for the play, so I should be pleased to have your description of it.

2. The lecture was a partial failure because the lecturer talked to the boys too rapidly in a high-pitched voice.

3. Dear Bertha, If you desire to have the joy of writing easily, you should practise reading the signs; then copy them from the page on to your writing paper till they flow readily. Failure at the beginning should not discourage you. Dismiss it from your thoughts. Go on trying. Stick to it; then you will be able to achieve your ambition. Yours truly,

4. Dear Sir, I have received your note. The boiler was dispatched to you by the national Road Services on the 10th. There was a brief delay owing to the registers at a depot in the east region having been mislaid, but the boiler should reach you with no more abnormal delay. Yours truly,

5. Dear Madam, Following the telephone call I received from Miss Roy, I am pleased to dispatch to you four copies of the schedules for which she asked. These should help you in your research. There is no charge for them. Yours truly,

LESSON 11

1. After giving the diet a fair trial, I am a good deal lighter.

2. What has been decided is that Mrs Dyer will read poems and play piano pieces when she appears on the radio.

3. Special precautions have been taken to obviate all risks of violation of the treaty.

4. The creation of fibres like rayon and nylon is a major branch of science in the textile business.

5. The spread of bacteria will normally be less in areas in which the air is drier.

6. Most large businesses have been putting in special appliances to expedite billing and the handling of mail.

7. Miss Pryor finished that job speedily and in a decidedly businesslike fashion.

8. Our Association has decided to open a library in each area with a librarian in charge.

9. You cannot secure tax reliefs

by creating an excessive depreciation charge on these assets.

10. Dear Sirs, Our radiator is what you need. It has a dial of small diameter on the side with which you can secure all the variations of heat radiation that are desired. Call and see it. Yours truly,

LESSON 12

1. Mr Byers declares that he should be able to repay the loan by the end of this year as he will then have ample resources.

2. An exhibition of rayon materials has been arranged for May 14 to 21 at the Main Hall, Olympia.

3. I am glad to send you the enclosed leaflet which describes and explains the O'Brian steam radiators.

4. Dear George, My clerk is rearranging the three lists of Associates and will send them to you in a day or so. I should be very glad if you could let me have a copy of the names on the original register. Yours truly,

5. Dear Sirs, In reply to your letter of May 18 about pictures for your journal, it is with regret that I must decline your offer. I think I should be able to take on more work for you later in the year when I may not be so busy. Yours truly,

6. Dear Madam, Your hair drier has been received at our works, and I am pleased to tell you that only a very small thing was at fault. It was easily put right; therefore our firm are not sending you a bill for this repair. Yours truly,

7. Dear Sir, In response to your letter, I shall be glad to see to it that packages addressed to you here in error are speedily readdressed and dispatched to you. Yours truly,

CHAPTER 3

LESSON 13

1. These premises cannot be let before the repair work on the roof and the rear rooms is finished.

2. Does this apparatus work by suction?

3. It is lucky that the missing enclosure was traced after you looked through the files.

4. Do you think the colour illustrations for this book can be ready for reproduction in a day or so?

5. Mrs Cook gladly agreed to the change of route for our Middle East tour.

6. In the typing pool Miss Hook wrote a couple of letters for me and the rough draft of a chapter for my book.

7. The food you eat should not exclude fruit, and it is better not to cook it.

8. Dear Madam, I have received your letter asking for a copy of our leaflet on fruit growing. This is enclosed, and I am sending with it our booklet that deals specially with pruning. Yours truly,

9. Dear Sir, The production in our works is mostly of ovens and cookers. Each worker in the group receives pay at the full rate plus a bonus for higher production. Yours truly,

LESSON 14

1. Most of the workers here get wages above the average for other trades in this area.
2. The swollen river was washing across the road, thus adding to our other worries, so we decided to take the west route.
3. When Walter goes with us to Westlake, we shall try to get him to take up swimming.
4. Can you let me know whether there is whale oil in this food preparation, and, if so, whether I ought to exclude it from my diet?
5. We gather that the worst cases are mostly occurring on highway A3, and have decided to arrange for that highway to be specially watched.
6. Dear Sirs, We could fit wash basins in all the upper rooms in either white or green enamel. May we call to see you about this at noon or after 4 on March 15? Yours truly,
7. Dear Madam, As you know, the makers of woollen clothing say there is nothing like wool for warmth and that it wears well. We enclose our leaflet about the woven sweaters that we can offer you. We think that it would be wise for you to get in early stocks of these sweaters. Yours truly,

LESSON 15

1. I have to be away during most of March, but will see you the next day after I return.
2. Mr Waters is satisfied to await the diagnosis of our doctor.
3. He believes that it is necessary these days for youth to be wide awake and go-ahead in its aims and desires.
4. If you are not satisfied with these yarns, you may return them at our expense and we will try to give you satisfaction.
5. Messrs Quick Bros. are to quote on the basis that the Broadway will be built with twin roadways having a separating wall in the middle.
6. To live satisfactorily, let each day have its quota of quiet thought and reading.
7. We shall requisition another 25 squares of the material. When these are delivered and made up, the yacht will be fully equipped.
8. Dear Sirs, In reply to your letter, it is my belief that the other firm of weavers whose address I enclose would be able to satisfy your need for quicker delivery of the yellow yarns. Yours truly,
9. Dear Madam, I have received your note. Yes, I am aware that a query has been raised about the worth of the liquid soap; yet I believe you will not be dissatisfied with it. Yours truly,

LESSON 16

1. I trust that you will be able to bring Mrs Judge with you to these

evening functions we are running in the spring.
2. Dr Banker gave Frank something to drink before dealing with his crushed finger.
3. The plumber arrived after lunch, bringing his mate, who had to rush back for the tools to repair our water tank.
4. I believe we can make the young people's social go with a swing, though I know there is much to be done both before and after the fun has begun.
5. When you retire, our scheme gives you the right to take a single lump sum if you prefer this.
6. Dear Sirs, We have reserved for you in our Summer Issue a column next to a special feature. We could accept a line block 3″ square from the Lion Brush people to fill a blank in the fourth column of page 15. Yours truly,
7. Dear Sir, Come to the King's Head Hotel in the spring or summer. A warm welcome awaits you whether your stay is lengthy or only for some days. Yours truly,

LESSON 17

1. Firms in the building trade are registered among the other records kept by our company.
2. Miss Field has appeared twice in the top place and has not been below third in the award lists.
3. I desire to record our thanks especially to the older children who helped so greatly in arranging the display.
4. Mr Long understood that the border should be folded over where shown on the chart that you prepared.
5. The truth cannot be ignored that nowhere are the people shouldering a greater burden of taxation than here.
6. Under these old-fashioned bookkeeping methods the work takes a great deal longer, and they should be discarded.
7. When you have filled up the enclosed card, it should be mailed to this address accompanied by your remittance.
8. I told Mr Hardy that these soiled copies may be sold at half-price.
9. Dear Sir, We thank you for your letter of May 25. In response, we shall remit by cheque the balance arising from the overcharge on hardware goods supplied to you in March. Yours truly,

LESSON 18

1. Dear Sirs, Thank you for the 15 yards of muslin that you secured for us from the sale of the assets of Cousins & Company. We were greatly in need of this material, and we appreciate very sincerely your help on this occasion. Yours truly,
2. Dear Madam, I shall have pleasure in sending you, if we have them still in stock, a dozen copies of the old issues of our school magazine describing the matches our teams have played this year. You will be pleased to

hear that our Principal has again asked Mr Younger to arrange our games fixtures for the next season. These will appear in the May issue of the magazine. Yours truly,
3. Dear Mr Bridges, Our Treasurer tells me that, if we are to avoid making a heavy loss on the year's working, drastic measures will have to be taken speedily. It will be necessary to cut expenses as well as to raise our returns from sales of finished materials. A meeting to discuss these measures is being called for the evening of the 18th. If you can be there, we shall all be glad. Yours truly,

CHAPTER 4

LESSON 19

1. Only 1 oz. of flour is used in this recipe.
2. The view of the weather bureau experts is that there will soon be much more cloud and some showers in the south.
3. Once a year we issue a review outlining the most important and advanced schemes for generating power.
4. No doubt the crowd admired the skill of those players who won their bouts, greeting them with loud cheers.
5. One thing of importance in this plan is that every voucher can be taken out quickly from the unit in which it is kept.
6. Have you ever been to the Peak near Derby? I am told there is a unique view from the top of it.
7. Dear Sir, Thank you for your letter of the 21st. It is true that there has been a dispute over the claim of the makers that their XL tubes can hold 40 cubic feet of liquid fuel, but this is a matter about which we are not prepared to argue. It would help us, though, to be told how much you are charged for fuel for your boilers—as a check on the prices that we are now paying our suppliers. Yours truly,

LESSON 20

1. The *Illustrated Weekly* can always be posted to any area in the world at the rates listed on the enclosed card.
2. We have noted with thanks your suggestion that the study notes be given in greater detail, but I fear we may be unable to adopt it.
3. Anyone in your family who wishes it can be admitted as a simple Member for only a nominal sum. Women as well as men can usually be accepted as Associates after satisfying our examiners and paying the higher fee.
4. Dear Sir, It is now several weeks since you suggested that United Cement shares would be worth buying. I adopted the suggestion and actually added to my holding, and have benefited greatly. I wish you to realise that the advice you gave is immensely appreciated. Yours truly,
5. Dear Sirs, The cases of fruit

you asked for have gone off to you today. If you wish to remit by return and not take the usual one month's credit, you may make a deduction of $2\frac{1}{2}\%$ from the enclosed bill. Yours truly,

LESSON 21

1. Make an entry in the index for each place named in the book.
2. It seemed that he was likely to be disappointed with the outcome of that venture because vacant possession of the premises couldn't be granted sufficiently early.
3. His small salary is earned and is exempt from taxation, but he will have to pay on his unearned return from shares.
4. A wide knowledge of current and recent events will help you to avoid blunders in your work.
5. When Mr Andrews learned about the risk of attack by armed raiders, he anticipated their arrival by establishing a trained guard for the protection of the plant.
6. We are well known printers and binders, and we guarantee to give satisfaction.
7. Dear Sir, After examining the details supplied by the several applicants, we have appointed Mr Bond to fill our staff vacancy. We find him a young man of brilliant intelligence, and we like his friendly manner. Thank you for your kindness in mentioning him. Yours truly,

LESSON 22

1. I have taken out various policies with the Union Mutual Assurance Company and have been well suited.
2. Numerous producers of manufactured goods have sent a large volume of their goods abroad—a much bigger volume than in previous years.
3. As jobs become vacant, there are excellent opportunities for girls to be appointed from the general office if they have rendered good service and shown intelligence.
4. The editor said that the final day for receiving copy is the 15th of the month preceding the date of issue. Naturally he didn't want all the copy to arrive at his office on that date!
5. Dear Sir, Next Tuesday morning, July 15, will see the opening of Newsom & Sons' new store for men. On the second floor you will find many bargains in men's suits made to individual measures. We feel that if you visit the new store you will not go away empty handed. You will have seized an opportunity and got what you really wanted without paying extra. We shall open at 9 o'clock in the morning and remain open till 7.0 o'clock. Yours truly,

LESSON 23

1. Perhaps it would be better if those old documents that are now on the ground floor were moved down to the basement.
2. In our view Mr Townley

showed excellent judgment in his appointments of personnel for the permanent staff.

3. The accountancy profession is one that gives scope for you to mount the ladder of promotion and achieve a prosperous career.

4. We are experimenting with an arrangement of light background colouring above a brown border round the walls.

5. At the price of only a half-crown, these workbooks with flexible binding prove readily saleable, and you will find them a soundly profitable line to stock.

6. Dear Sir, In reply to your letter of August 18, we are making an adjustment favourable to you in the percentage of discount on your bill, and we trust this will meet with your approval. We have to point out though that your previous balance is now overdue for payment, and we should appreciate a cheque by return in settlement. Failing this, a reasonable amount should be remitted on account before the end of this month. Yours truly,

LESSON 24

1. As you have the appropriate talents, I do seriously suggest that you prepare yourself to take up a political career.

2. For myself, it would be quite satisfactory if the announcement of his appointment to this responsible office were made next month.

3. An appreciable amount of the chemical had leaked through—sufficient to render the articles in the package no longer suitable for experimental work.

4. I myself was quite unable to account in any logical way for the occurrence of this mechanical trouble.

5. Our local paper announces that a capable woman is wanted to take over the secretaryship of the Essex County Musical Club.

6. It is only a few months since you yourself thought it advisable for us to have periodical assessments; yet on Tuesday afternoon you did not seem to be in agreement with me about this matter.

7. We think it is desirable that your wife should herself take out an endowment policy with the Union Life Assurance Company.

8. Dear Sir, Kindly fill up the relevant section of the enclosed document—relating to Fellowship, Associateship or Membership, whichever is applicable—and return it to the General Secretary with a remittance of the appropriate fee. The latter should be made payable to the Historical Association. Yours truly,

CHAPTER 5

LESSON 25

1. Since we have been unable to secure different sources of raw material supplies, it has been necessary to suspend accepting orders for our products.

2. The business executive must

use initiative in creating new opportunities for progress and expansion.

3. Dear Sir, I am happy to tell you that Mr Carpenter is making a scientific analysis of the problems relative to the development of our new device in practical style for marketing purposes. The details kindly given in your letter will enable him to proceed more rapidly with this urgent work, and we are most appreciative of the co-operative way in which you have responded to the appeal we made. Yours truly,

4. Dear Madam, Thank you for your letter. Several of the properties you mention are in streets situated in the division that is to be rebuilt under the County Council's development plan, and work to this end is now in progress. When speaking to members of the Council I shall suggest cogent reasons for deferring some sections of the scheme—among them the diversions that would disturb the flow of traffic. Yours truly,

LESSON 26

1. I must ask you to get the electric wiring done without delay at the International Hall, as I shall have another job for you very shortly.

2. The cablegram was handed to Dr Shortland during a game of bridge, but the message did not interfere with play for more than a few moments.

3. The family did all the interior decorations of the flat themselves. It was a fine co-operative enterprise to which they devoted several days of their summer holiday.

4. Dear Professor, I enclose a notice of a meeting of the Electronics Section of our Association to be held next month. After my short talk on the new enterprise we are undertaking, there will be an interval during which I wish to introduce Dr Carpenter to yourself and the other scientific executives. Another purpose of the meeting is to appoint a new electrician on our staff. I have myself interviewed Mr George Shorter, and you may know other electrical experts whom you would wish to nominate for this appointment.

LESSON 27

1. If I had been in the area myself a few days ago, I should have been able to do some worthwhile business. I wanted to see several people of importance to our company who were not available when I was there a few months ago.

2. Those people say they want to be granted an agency for our lines, but I wrote them not long ago pointing out that this was not possible.

3. Dear Sirs, Some weeks ago we wrote quoting our price for the repairs to your premises, and as soon as you let us have a reply we shall go ahead in accordance with your wishes. Please let us know if you want us to proceed now with the various other jobs you mentioned. Yours truly,

4. Dear Sir, Thank you for your order of June 19. Of course it is likely to take a few days for the goods to reach you by rail, but we hope that this will not entail any serious delay.

We wanted the articles listed in our order 513 to be delivered to Mr Johnson and not to ourselves. He wants them for a special display early next month, and we are sure you will desire to do the utmost that you can to help him in this matter. Yours truly

LESSON 28

1. Mr Spender says it is doubtful whether some of the Club's rules are useful now, and he is hopeful that the next meeting may agree to modifications that he will propose.

2. We hope that you will be able to give special priority to the enclosed order as we want the goods urgently. If you think you would not be entirely justified in giving it top priority, please be sure to let us have a majority of the articles as soon as possible.

3. Dear Leonard, I hope you will get the worthwhile job that you are seeking in the offices of your local authority. Perhaps it would be helpful to you if I wrote to Mr Gentry testifying to your abilities and personal qualities. If you would wish me to do so, just let me know. Yours truly,

4. Dear Sir, Two days ago on receipt of your order we carefully packed 200 Royal Tea sets, specification A12, and dispatched them for shipment to you by steamship "Charity." We are sure that with your facilities you will be able to sell this beautiful china to the majority of your buyers as trial orders that will lead, we hope, to worthwhile orders very soon. Yours truly,

LESSON 29

1. Dear Sirs, We are happy to testify that the new system of electric heating which you supplied for our building is much better than the temporary arrangement that it replaced, and is highly esteemed by our entire staff. Yours very truly,

2. Dear Mrs Cotton, We have not been able to obtain a precise match for the sample button that you sent, but we suggest that the buttons enclosed would be suitable for the costume you mention. Sincerely yours,

3. My dear Mr Fenton, I am sending you a carton of smoking mixture which should reach you to-morrow. Your acceptance of this as evidence of my thanks for your helpful co-operation would be warmly appreciated. I hope you will give me the opportunity of entertaining you to dinner when I next visit your city, which will be at no distant date. Yours very sincerely,

4. Gentlemen, Responding to your announcement in the Bulletin, I tender the attached record of my qualifications and previous appointments. As a student I attained a high standard in the customary training courses, and I append details. Yours respectfully,

LESSON 30

1. An understanding of that system seems to me extraordinarily difficult to obtain. I don't know why some terms are used or what they mean. Though I have tried several times, the difficulty remains.

2. When the merchandise that we purchased from your department store was received on Thursday, we found one carton damaged. This package has been returned so that you may determine what replacements to make. No doubt you will claim in the ordinary way from the Western Express Company.

3. Dear Mr Turner, We enclose tickets for your tour. Your party will be escorted by Mr and Mrs Merchant, and will depart from Waterloo at 12 noon. Arrival at Southampton is timed to meet the steamship Southern Bell, which leaves for St Peter Port at 3 o'clock. The journey terminates at the Northern Hotel, which is a quarter of an hour by coach from St Peter Port. In case of difficulty, or if this itinerary must for any extraordinary reason be varied, please turn for guidance to your escorts. Yours faithfully,

CHAPTER 6

LESSON 31

1. I have pleasure in attesting that Miss Mary Morris has been an assistant in our Accounts Department for the last four years, and that we have always found her thoroughly reliable and honest. She takes the active personal interest that never neglects any aspect of her work.

2. Businessmen do not select attractive applicants for posts irrespective of their ability or past record. These will be rejected if their attempts in the tests given are below the highest standard.

3. Dear Sirs, The enclosed list of our latest products will interest you. It offers the finest quality with the lowest prices of any merchandise of this type now available. Yours truly,

4. Dear Mr Tennent, You will be interested and pleased to know that we have effected the sale of your property in Western Avenue. The prospect of our being able to do so seemed rather remote, as we have been earnestly seeking a purchaser for the past five months. But your property has now been bought by the largest firm of merchants in this district. Their remittance for the sale price, from which we have deducted our charges, is enclosed. Yours sincerely,

LESSON 32

1. Thank you for asking me to attend your next meeting. I shall be present as your Association is a body whose aims and activities I have never ceased to hold in the greatest possible respect.
2. Gentlemen, I notice your advertisement in *The Times* of September 4, and that you wish to consider applications for the post of representative in the Eastern Counties. As the advertisement was rather brief, I should be obliged if you would send me the fullest details in order that I may determine whether I should make application or seek a different type of appointment elsewhere. Yours respectfully,
3. The chairman said: I am happy to state that in the last year we have extended our factories to meet the demand for our latest product. Turnover has bounded to a new high record, and your Board have decided to recommend a dividend of 15 per cent on the Ordinary shares. You will probably remember that last year we started a scheme by which our workers participate in the dividends paid. Their share now amounts to 20 per cent of the total. We are satisfied that this participation by the staff is in the best interests of the Company.

LESSON 33

1. These carpets are of a very superior quality, and we suggest you would not be wise if you postponed your decision to order a supply.
2. Our books will be closed for the period December 16 to January 7 inclusive, and during this period share transfers cannot be accepted.
3. As a means of closing this transaction, we agree to accept from you a cheque postdated to the end of the present month.
4. In the Post Office Guide you will find the postage rates to all parts of the world, and it includes a full list of the offices in which postal business is transacted.
5. We are now stocking a series of post cards showing superb views of local scenery in colour.
6. Dear Mr Hindes, I am unable at the moment to answer your query about the latest television transmitters, but if the desired details are obtained by the time this letter is dispatched they will be included in a postscript. Yours sincerely,
7. Mr Hughes: On account of the inclement weather, I suggest that your trip be postponed a few days. R. J. Williams.

LESSON 34

1. I am slightly embarrassed to find there are places in the Empire that are unknown to me. I must concentrate on them.

2. Dear Miss Temple, I am glad that you have enrolled for shorthand in the evening classes and are enthusiastic. I know that Miss O'Connor will give you every encouragement, and you should have completed the Manual by the end of the session. Plenty of reading practice each day will impress the outlines on your mind, and you will soon be able to write with accuracy and transcribe perfectly. Yours very sincerely,

3. Dear Mrs Conway, I was present at the concert arranged by the Young Conservatives last Friday night. Usually I do not enjoy concerts given by young people, and I went there expecting to be entertained in an amused sort of way. I know now how unfair that expectation was, for they gave an accomplished rendering of each item, and the contents of the programme were of an exacting nature. It should not be inferred from this that their playing was perfect; it would be unreasonable to expect that. But I was greatly impressed by their talent. Yours sincerely,

LESSON 35

1. A printer's error or a typing mistake often results from the transposition of two letters.

2. I presume that there will be no difficulty in your accepting the proposition set out in my letter of July 12.

3. A famous politician once said his Party was going "onward and upward," but those who were in opposition thought it right to assume that his policy only led backward.

4. It may be presumed that the awkward disposition displayed by young Edward may be traceable to difficulties in his training in boyhood, and even back into early childhood.

5. The multiple stores have recently opened several branches in our neighbourhood, and I am told that more will be established when they find shopkeepers willing to dispose of their existing tenancies.

6. Dear Sirs, Our present position is such that we are unable to undertake fresh commitments until our current programme is completed. Afterwards we hope to resume operations on an increased scale, and we shall then consult you about the various propositions that you mention in your letter. Yours faithfully,

LESSON 36

1. Dear Mrs Allwood, For several evenings Ann had been busy at her writing with quantities of paper; and, when approached, she assumed an air of secrecy. Today she published her first number of a magazine for girls at the price of 1d. We were suitably impressed, offered her our congratulations, and gladly acknowledged the excellence of the new publication.

This issue has numerous fashion drawings, some advertisements, an accumulation of clippings, some surprisingly ingenious recipes, and a column of speculations concerning the future through the medium of the stars!

The one copy produced so far has a circulation of four readers, so the income seemingly will not rise above 4d. Doubtless the four would wish to become regular readers, and Dad has made offerings of ideas in the hope of stimulating the production of at least a second number. Yet Ann seems disinclined to allow any interference in her one-man show. Perhaps ultimately staff will have to be engaged and the number of copies increased to keep pace with the demand.

I know you are interested in Ann's doings, and I hope that, when you next visit us, you may be allowed to become a reader—upon payment of 1d. in advance. This would help to improve the financial situation of the journal!

Yours very sincerely,

CHAPTER 7

LESSON 37

1. We have received a communication from the circulation department indicating that the next issue of the journal will include a duplicated list of back numbers available.

2. Our Institute appointed a committee to investigate and present their views on methods of modifying the constitution in ways calculated to make our proceedings more effective.

3. Please communicate your decision to us as soon as the investigations on which you are working have been completed.

4. We reciprocate your good wishes, and thank you for your helpful attitude in clearing up the confusion that arose.

5. Enrolment for this course of study will place you under no obligation to recommend or advocate the system used.

6. When my daughter wanted to substitute domestic science for geometry in her entry for the General Certificate of Education I refused to permit this. I offered an increase in her allocation of pocket money if she worked harder at the problems she found confusing. The results showed she had lacked persistence rather than aptitude.

LESSON 38

1. After frequent complaints had been made, an Enquiry into the operations of the syndicate was instituted, and in consequence of the report by the chairman of that Enquiry a full investigation has now been ordered by the Minister.

2. I am aware that this patient has neuritis; yet it seems that her real difficulty is a psychological rather than a physiological one.

3. Dear Sirs, I regret that communications on the Eastern section have been interrupted by the unofficial rail strike. Consequently, we have now been able to make arrangements for distribution by road, and the goods you ordered a few weeks ago should reach you in about ten days. We apologise for the delay. Yours faithfully,

4. Dear Mr Jennings, My apologies are tendered for the refusal to sign a copy of the certificate awarded by the society to Mrs M. Brown in February of last year. Evidently I had not adequately studied the requirements drawn up subsequently. I should now be happy to add my signature to this copy. Yours very sincerely,

LESSON 39

1. In confirmation of our telephone message, we enclose our quotation for the stationery supplies listed in your letter. We trust that we shall receive your order for these materials at your early convenience.

2. Plenty of repetition practice will assist you in the consolidation of your knowledge of the principles.

3. Dear Dr Hastings, Early next year we shall require to print a second edition of your *Introduction to Philosophy*. Will you kindly give some preliminary thought to any additions, omissions, or other changes that may be in your estimation desirable and incorporate them in a memorandum to us before the end of this year. As the present edition contains a convenient number of pages for printing in sections of 16, we should like you to ensure, if possible, that additions to the text are offset by equivalent omissions so that the total length of the book is not changed. Failing that, the addition of another complete 16-page section or even more than one would not be seriously inconvenient. Perhaps you will be so good as to keep this explanation in mind when working on the next revised edition of your book. Yours sincerely,

LESSON 40

1. Dear Sir, As announced in the newspapers, our furniture stores have been reorganized and extended to cover almost two acres of floor space. A substantial part of our stock is offered at prices anyone can afford; but there is nevertheless a further section containing stylish furniture that appeals to those with the larger incomes. Irrespective of the price you pay, you will be convinced by experience that exceedingly good value is given at our stores. Indeed, our reputation is built on that. Yours truly,

2. Dear Reader, You are hereby reminded that you may renew your subscription to *Home and Family* magazine in the month of December, or, alternatively, you may send us the full and correct addresses of three new subscribers and receive a free renewal subscription to cover fifteen months. A substantial number of readers have already elected to do so. The more subscribers we get, the better value we shall be able to give; and it helps our organisation to receive subscriptions early. I enclose a self-addressed envelope and three forms for use by your friends. Kindest regards, Yours sincerely,

LESSON 41

1. I am glad to know that the discussion you had with our representative has established a friendly understanding and the means to prevent misunderstandings from arising in the future.

2. Will you please see that this work is brought up to date during the next week or two.

3. One of the most important factors in our line of business is the creation of a better understanding between the workers and the management.

4. In order to become a professional shorthand-writer, you must thoroughly understand the principles; you should also practise regularly every day for a few minutes at least.

5. Dear Madam, Thank you for your letter of October 27. It is unfortunate that we misunderstood your wishes, but I am glad to have the assurance that our error has been rectified now in such a way as to meet with your approval. Your confirmation of this is very much appreciated. Yours truly,

6. Dear Sirs, During the past two or three years we have been using your paper on some of our fast-running printing presses, and I should like to say that it has proved to be one of the best grades of paper that we have ever used. You will understand that we regard this product as one of the finest of its kind now on the market, and one that we are always happy to recommend to our friends in the trade. Yours sincerely,

LESSON 42

1. Probably nowhere else in the world has there been so splendid an occasion as the Coronation of Queen Elizabeth II. This event and the subsequent series of Commonwealth tours which evoked wonderful expressions of loyalty and affection are likely to have produced some of the most far-reaching and beneficial results, not only for us in this kingdom, but throughout the world.

2. Dear Mr Everett, I have now received your report on the Johnson case and am at a loss to understand why you decided to delegate this important and personal matter to someone else even though he is a person of substantial rank. The directions given to you throughout the proceedings were, I should have thought, explicit and unquestionable. I am wondering whether you have some explanation that would be satisfactory to your superiors. Yours sincerely,

3. In the course of his comments the Chairman said: You will understand that during the past year your directors were confronted by what seemed to be a multitude of difficulties. Many of these, however, have been overcome, and I am of the opinion that, despite the further difficulties that may confront us in the future, we shall be able to direct our course into more or less smooth waters—if not immediately, then before very long. I should like to say also that your Board has received wonderful assistance from everybody at head office and throughout the organisation.

CHAPTER 8

LESSON 43

1. Several hundred people were present at Chamber of Commerce House on June 22. Before the meeting concluded, they expressed their confidence in the Council of the Society by re-electing its members as a body.

2. Your comments on the subject are noted, and we have no objection to adopting the scheme to which you refer, especially since you are confident that it will effectively promote the object that we have in view.

3. Dear Mr Barnes, With reference to the suggestion contained in your letter of November 18, I have come to the conclusion, after considering the whole subject very carefully, that we should purchase the adjoining houses as well as the central property and convert them into dwellings suitable for small households. The success of such a venture is practically guaranteed by the extent of the existing demand for accommodation of this type. Yours sincerely,

4. Dear Sirs, We enclose particulars of our latest weed-killing mixture. This sells to the public at 2s. per pound, and we are able to supply it to retail dealers in quantities of not less than 10 cwt at the special price of £5 per cwt, delivered direct from our warehouse. Yours faithfully,

LESSON 44

1. The railway strike starting yesterday in Bradford has spread to several other districts. It may not be possible to recognize all the men's claims as justified, but there must be some recognition to facilitate a settlement.

2. Dear George, When I was working in the Correspondence Department, I found that my ability to write down rapidly in shorthand the names of people and places was a valuable asset. For instance, we frequently wrote to Mr Cunningham, a retail dealer in Maryport; to Mrs Wakefield, who owned a newspaper and stationery shop in

Rochester; and to Messrs Hatfield & Sons, manufacturers in Accrington. We would also write to our various representatives—to Arthur Greenfield, who covered the Peterborough district, to John Devonport, of the Colchester area, etc. Occasionally we wrote to places abroad; for instance, to Mr Gainsborough, our agent at Washington. You will find it a great advantage if you also develop your skill in writing personal and place names rapidly in shorthand. Yours sincerely,

LESSON 45

1. In a free country such as America, Canada, or Great Britain, the citizens exercise self-government through their elected representatives. In some other states the governing circles possess supreme power and freedom for the remainder of the population is greatly restricted.

2. About 100 years ago the U.K. was the world's chief importing and exporting country famous for the quality and character of its products. Its principal ports were London, Liverpool, and Bristol in England; Glasgow in Scotland; Belfast in Ireland. Great Britain is now exceeded in volume of trade by the U.S.A. and possibly the U.S.S.R.

3. Dear Mr Radford, When our representative Mr Rockingham was prosecuted for dangerous driving in consequence of his mishap on the North Circular Road last September, legal assistance was provided by the Automobile Association. His car had run off the road owing to a defect in the steering mechanism; and part of the case for the prosecution was that the vehicle was not mechanically in roadworthy condition. In this instance, however, there was no conclusive evidence that the defect had created trouble before or that Mr Rockingham must necessarily have been aware of its existence. In recognition of this fact and of the satisfactory character of Mr Rockingham's previous record, he was subjected only to a small fine. Although he was not physically injured, it is unfortunate that the nervous shock resulting from this accident has adversely affected his health, and he has now taken up a position with a firm in Manchester—one that does not require the use of a car. Otherwise we should have been glad to retain his services. Yours very sincerely,

PRINTED IN GREAT BRITAIN BY OFFSET LITHOGRAPHY BY
BILLING & SONS LTD, GUILDFORD, LONDON AND WORCESTER